The Gallup Poll
Cumulative Index

The Gallup Poll Cumulative Index

Public Opinion, 1998–2007

Edited by

Alec M. Gallup and Frank Newport

ROWMAN & LITTLEFIELD PUBLISHERS, INC.
Lanham • Boulder • New York • Toronto • Plymouth, UK

ROWMAN & LITTLEFIELD PUBLISHERS, INC.

Published in the United States of America
by Rowman & Littlefield Publishers, Inc.
A wholly owned subsidiary of The Rowman & Littlefield Publishing Group, Inc.
4501 Forbes Boulevard, Suite 200, Lanham, Maryland 20706
www.rowmanlittlefield.com

Estover Road
Plymouth PL6 7PY
United Kingdom

Copyright © 2008 by Rowman & Littlefield Publishers, Inc.

All rights reserved. No part of this publication may be reproduced, stored in a retrieval system, or transmitted in any form or by any means, electronic, mechanical, photo-copying, recording, or otherwise, without the prior permission of the publisher.

British Library Cataloguing in Publication Information Available

Library of Congress Cataloging-in-Publication Data:

The gallup poll cumulative index : public opinion, 1998–2007 / edited by Alec M. Gallup and Frank Newport.
    p. cm.
  ISBN-13: 978-0-7425-6314-8 (cloth : alk. paper)
  ISBN-10: 0-7425-6314-6 (cloth : alk. paper)
  ISBN-13: 978-0-7425-6592-0 (electronic)
  ISBN-10: 0-7425-6592-0 (electronic)
    1. Public opinion—United States—Indexes. 2. Social surveys—United States—Indexes. I. Gallup, Alec. II. Newport, Frank.
HN90.P8G355 2008
303.3'8097303—dc22   2008030917

Printed in the United States of America

♾™ The paper used in this publication meets the minimum requirements of American National Standard for Information Sciences—Permanence of Paper for Printed Library Materials, ANSI/NISO Z39.48-1992.

ABOUT THE AUTHORS

ALEC M. GALLUP is chairman of The Gallup Poll in the United States, and chairman of The Gallup Organization Ltd. in Great Britain, Europe, Gallup China, and Gallup Hungary. He has been employed by Gallup since 1959 and has directed or played key roles in many of the company's most ambitious and innovative projects. Areas of responsibility have focused on sampling procedures, question development and design, and analysis and reporting. Survey projects have included the following: Survey of Nine Islamic Nations, Global Cities Project, Global Survey on Attitudes Towards AIDS, The Health of The Planet Survey, Survey of Consumer Attitudes and Lifestyles in China, Human Needs and Satisfactions, and The Annual Survey of The Public's Attitudes Toward the Public Schools.

Gallup's educational background includes undergraduate work at Princeton University and the University of Iowa. He undertook graduate work in communications and journalism at Stanford University, and studied marketing and advertising research at New York University. His publications include *The Great American Success Story* (with George Gallup, Jr., Dow Jones-Irwin, 1986), "Death Penalty Sentiment in the United States" (with Hans Zeisel, *Journal of Quantitative Criminology*, 1989), *Presidential Approval: A Source Book* (with George Edwards, Johns Hopkins University Press, 1990), *The Gallup Poll Cumulative Index: Public Opinion 1935-1997*, Scholarly Resources, 1999), and *British Political Opinion 1937-2000: The Gallup Polls* (with Anthony King and Robert Wybrow, Politicos Publishing, 2001).

FRANK NEWPORT is editor-in-chief of The Gallup Poll in Princeton, New Jersey, and is in charge of the nation's best-known and longest-running continuous monitor of American public opinion. The Gallup Poll conducts over

40,000 interviews each year, and partners with USA Today in providing up to the minute polling on political and topical issues.

Dr. Newport is vice president of the National Council on Public Polls, a member of Executive Council of the American Association of Public Opinion Research, and is on the board of the Roper Center for Public Opinion Research. He is the author of *Polling Matters: Why Leaders Must Listen to the Wisdom of the People* (Warner Books, 2004), the coauthor with Stuart Rothenberg of *The Evangelical Voter*, and contributed to Where America Stands book series, *The Ethnic Voter* and *Ethnic Voters and National Issues*. His articles and op-eds have appeared in many publications, including the *American Sociological Review*, *Public Opinion Quarterly*, the *New York Times*, and the *Los Angeles Times*.

Newport has a B.A. from Baylor University, and an M.A. and Ph.D. in sociology from the University of Michigan. He moved to Princeton to take his current position at Gallup in 1990.

Frank Newport appears regularly on radio and television and he is the on-air host of Gallup's daily web-cast program "The Daily Briefing" at galluppoll.com, which is also podcast on iTunes. He is author of the blog feature "Gallup Guru" on USAToday.com and appears regularly on MSNBC and CNBC.

CONTENTS

Acknowledgments, **ix**

Introduction

    About the Index, **xi**

    Contents of the Collection, **xii**

    About the Gallup Poll, **xiii**

Gallup Poll Accuracy Records

    Presidential Elections, **xv**

    Congressional Elections, **xvi**

    Gallup Poll Sampling Procedures, **xviii**

Gallup Poll Cumulative Index, 1998–2007, **1**

ACKNOWLEDGMENTS

The *Gallup Poll Cumulative Index* is the result of the efforts of many talented and dedicated individuals. At Gallup we wish to express our gratitude to James Clifton, President and CEO; Jeffrey Jones, Managing Editor of the Gallup Poll; Lydia Saad, Senior Editor of the Gallup Poll; and Maura Strausberg, Data Librarian. Judith Keneman, Executive Assistant to the Editor in Chief and Production Editor of *The Gallup Poll Briefing Magazine* deserves special recognition for supervising the compilation, editing and publishing of the last 9 volumes of the Gallup Poll collection, as well as this volume.

Fred L. Israel, retired professor at City University of New York, also deserves our thanks and appreciation. Over twenty-five years ago he conceived the *Gallup Poll Public Opinion* series and convinced Dr. George Gallup of its merit. He personally compiled the first 25 volumes in the *Gallup Poll* collection.

A.M.G.
F.N.

INTRODUCTION

About the Index

The Gallup Poll Cumulative Index is a comprehensive index to *The Gallup Poll: Public Opinion,* series for the years 1998–2007. This collection of thirty-four volumes is the largest compilation of public opinion findings ever published and one of the largest reference sets produced on any subject.

This addition of a second volume to the *Cumulative Index 1935-1997* already published enables researchers to readily access the attitudes and opinions of Americans concerning virtually every national and international issue and event from Franklin D. Roosevelt's presidency through 2007. More specifically, readers can quickly and easily find the results of the more than **85,000** questions that the Gallup Poll—the world's oldest and most respected public opinion poll—has asked of the American public over the past seven decades. Results of the survey questions are shown for the nearly 10,000 Gallup Poll reports reproduced in the thirty-four volume collection. These reports have been released to the national media on a continuous one-to-four times per week basis since October 20, 1935. Because almost every report is based on multiple survey questions, the results of questions related to the desired one are also readily accessible.

In addition to providing the results of survey questions for the nation as a whole, the Gallup Reports show the following:

- breakdowns of the results by key demographics (for example, gender, age, education, political affiliation, and region;
- opinion trends, which show the results of questions that have been previously asked; and
- since 1972, all or most of the text appearing in the original reports.

Technical details concerning how the surveys were conducted are also described, including sample size, interviewing method, and interviewing dates. Arranged alphabetically, main topics are indicated in bold. Abbreviated survey questions then follow under each major topic. Articles, conjunctions, prepositions, and pronouns are usually not included in the alphabetization of survey questions. The years in which questions were asked are also indicated in bold, followed by page numbers that refer to the specific *Gallup Poll: Public Opinion* volume in which the complete survey question and respondents' answers can be found.

Contents of the Collection

The thirty-four volume *Gallup Poll: Public Opinion* collection documents public opinion from 1935 to the present in the following five separate and distinct areas.

Recording the Public's Response to Major News Events. Gallup has recorded the public's attitudes and opinions in response to every major news event of the last seven decades. Examples include Adolf Hitler's invasion of the Soviet Union, the bombing of Pearl Harbor, the dropping of the atomic bomb on Hiroshima, the assassination of President John F. Kennedy, the moon landing, the taking of U.S. hostages in Iran, the World Trade Center bombing, the Tiananmen Square massacre, the O. J. Simpson trial verdict, the impeachment of President Bill Clinton, the September 11, 2001, terrorist bombings and the Iraq War.

Measuring the Strength of Support for the President, Political Candidates, and Political Parties. For over seventy years, Gallup has measured, on a continuous basis, the strength of support for the President, for the congressional opposition, and for various political candidates and parties in national elections. This is the role most closely associated with Gallup in the public's mind.

Tracking the Public's Attitudes Concerning Enduring Societal Issues. Since 1935, Gallup has tracked the public's attitudes and opinions concerning a wide range of enduring societal issues, including such narrowly defined issues as abortion and capital punishment as well as broader, multifaceted issues such as crime, the environment, and education. Most of Gallup's long-term subjective social indicators, which are designed to measure social, political, and economic attitudinal trends, are contributed by this category.

Revealing American Lifestyle Trends. Another on-going Gallup polling activity has been to document American lifestyles, including periodic measurements of participation in a wide range of leisure activities and other pursuits. Additional examples include frequent series describing the public's tastes and favorites in various areas, and their knowledge level as revealed by national "quizzes" in geography, history, science, politics, and the like.

Gauging and Charting the Public's Mood. From its earliest days the Gallup Poll has sought to determine, on an on-going basis, Americans' satisfaction—or dissatisfaction—with the direction in which the nation appeared to be headed and with the way they thought that their personal lives were progressing. This process also has involved regular assessment of the people's mood regarding the state of the nation's economy, as well as with the status of their personal finances, their jobs, and other aspects of their lives.

About the Gallup Poll

Two of the most frequently asked questions concerning the Gallup Poll are:

Who pays for or provides financial support to the Poll? And who determines which topics are covered by the Poll or, more specifically, who decides which questions are asked on Gallup surveys? Since its founding in 1935 the Gallup Poll has been underwritten by the nation's daily newspapers, which pay for the Gallup Poll column on a syndicated or shared cost basis. In recent years, funding also has come from the national daily newspaper *USA Today*, with whom Gallup conducts the *USA Today*/Gallup Poll.

Suggestions for poll questions come from Gallup's media subscribers, from other print and broadcast media, and from institutions as well as from individuals, including members of Congress and other public officials, university professors, and foundation executives. In addition, the public itself is regularly questioned about the problems and issues facing the nation as they perceive them. Their answers establish priorities and provide an up-to-the-minute list of topic areas to explore through the Poll.

Although columnists, editorial writers, and reporters have historically attempted to assess and report public opinion without the benefit of objective data, these efforts have been, by definition, subjective and less than impartial. The advent of the scientific polls in the mid-1930s added an important new dimension to news reporting: the ability to describe accurately and impartially how the public viewed or felt about a news event or national issue. From this time forth, the news media could report "public opinion"—in effect, what people thought as well as what people did—with some measure of confidence.

Not surprisingly, the initial efforts of the new scientific opinion polls were met with skepticism from all quarters. Critics questioned, for example, how it was possible to determine the opinions of the entire American populace based on only 1,000 interviews or less, or how one knew whether people were telling the truth. The credibility of the new polls was enhanced significantly, however, when Gallup correctly predicted that Franklin D. Roosevelt would win the 1936 presidential election in a landslide, a prediction that directly contradicted the forecast of the Literary Digest Poll, the poll of record at that time. The Digest Poll, which was not based on scientific sampling procedures, claimed that FDR's Republican challenger, Alfred Landon, would easily win the election. Over the subsequent seven decades the scientifically based opinion polls have gained a level of acceptance to where they are used today to investigate virtually every aspect of human experience in most nations of the world. To a large degree, this acceptance is due to the record of accuracy achieved by the polls in pre-election surveys. These tests of candidate strength or "trial heats," which were introduced by Gallup in the 1930s (along with the presidential "approval" ratings), demonstrated that scientific survey techniques can accurately quantify public sentiment. For example, in the sixteen presidential elections since 1936, the deviation between Gallup's final pre-election survey figures and the actual election results is 2.2% and, since 1960, only 1.5%. Correspondingly, in the fifteen midterm congressional elections measured since 1936, the deviation between Gallup's final pre-election survey figures and the actual election results is 1.5%.

Alec M. Gallup
Frank Newport

GALLUP POLL ACCURACY RECORD

Presidential Elections

	Candidates	Final Gallup Survey	Election Result	Gallup Deviation
2004	Bush	49	51	-2
	Kerry	49	48	1
	Other	2	1	1
2000	Gore	46	48.4	-2.4
	Bush	48	47.9	0.1
	Nader	4	2.7	1.3
	Buchanan	1	0.4	0.6
	Other	1	0.6	0.4
1996	Clinton	52	49.2	2.8
	Dole	41	40.9	0.1
	Perot	7	8.5	-1.5
1992	Clinton	49	43	6
	Bush	37	37.5	-0.5
	Perot	14	18.9	-4.9
1988	Bush	56	53.4	2.6
	Dukakis	44	45.7	-1.7
1984	Reagan	59	58.8	0.2
	Mondale	41	40.6	0.4
1980	Reagan	47	50.8	-3.8
	Carter	44	41	3
	Anderson	8	6.6	1.4
	Other	1	1.6	-0.6
1976	Carter	48	50.1	-2.1
	Ford	49	48	1
	McCarthy	2	0.9	1.1
	Other	1	0.9	0.1

Presidential Elections (continued)

	Candidates	*Final Gallup Survey*	*Election Result*	*Gallup Deviation*
1972	Nixon	62	60.7	1.3
	McGovern	38	37.6	0.4
1968	Nixon	43	43.4	-0.4
	Humphrey	42	42.7	-0.7
	Wallace	15	13.5	1.5

Midterm Congressional Elections

			Demo-crat %	*Repub-lican* %	*Other/ Undecided* %	*Dem. Advan-tage* %
2006	Nov 2-5	Likely Voters	51.0	44.0	5.0	7.0
		Actual	53.0	45.0	3.3	8.0
		2-Pty Vote	54.1	45.9	—	8.2
2002	Oct 31-Nov 3	Likely Voters	45.0	51.0	4.0	-6.0
		Actual	**45.9**	**50.5**	**3.3**	**-4.6**
		2-Pty Vote	**47.6**	**52.4**	—	**-4.8**
1998	Oct 29-Nov 1	Likely Voters	49.0	45.0	6.0	4.0
		Actual	**47.8**	**48.4**	**3.8**	**-0.6**
		2-Pty Vote	**49.7**	**50.3**	—	**-0.6**
1994	Nov 2-6	Likely Voters	46.5	53.5	0.0	-7.0
		Actual	**45.5**	**52.4**	**2.1**	**-6.9**
		2-Pty Vote	**46.5**	**53.5**	—	**-7.0**
1990	Oct 25-28	Likely Voters	54.0	46.0	0.0	8.0
		Actual	**52.9**	**44.9**	**2.2**	**8.0**
		2-Pty Vote	**54.1**	**45.9**	—	**8.2**
1986	Oct 24-27	Likely Voters	—	—	—	—
		Registered Voters	52.0	40.0	0.0	12.0
		Actual	**54.6**	**44.5**	**0.9**	**10.1**
		2-Pty Vote	**55.1**	**44.9**	—	**10.2**

1982	Oct 15-18/					
Sep 17-20		Likely Voters	55.0	45.0	0.0	10.0
Final results based on		**Actual**	**55.3**	**43.1**	**1.6**	**12.2**
combined studies		**2-Pty Vote**	**56.2**	**43.8**	**—**	**12.4**
1978	Oct 27-30/					
Oct 13-16		Likely Voters	55.0	45.0	0.0	10.0
Final results based on		**Actual**	**53.7**	**44.9**	**1.4**	**8.8**
combined studies		**2-Pty Vote**	**54.5**	**45.5**	**—**	**8.9**
1974	Oct 18-21	Likely Voters	60.0	40.0	0.0	20.0
		Actual	**57.6**	**40.6**	**1.8**	**17.0**
		2-Pty Vote	**58.7**	**41.3**	**—**	**17.3**
1970	Oct 26-31	Likely Voters	53.0	47.0	0.0	6.0
		Actual	**53.4**	**45.1**	**1.5**	**8.3**
		2-Pty Vote	**54.2**	**45.8**	**—**	**8.4**
1966	Oct 31-Nov 5	Likely Voters	52.5	47.5	0.0	5.0
		Actual	**50.9**	**48.3**	**0.8**	**2.6**
		2-Pty Vote	**51.3**	**48.7**	**—**	**2.6**
1962	Oct 29-Nov 2	Likely Voters	55.5	45.5	0.0	10.0
		Actual	**52.5**	**47.2**	**0.3**	**5.3**
		2-Pty Vote	**52.7**	**47.3**	**—**	**5.3**
1958	Oct 26-31	Likely Voters	57.0	43.0	0.0	14.0
		Actual	**56.2**	**43.4**	**0.4**	**12.8**
		2-Pty Vote	**56.4**	**43.6**	**—**	**12.9**
1954	Oct 26-30	Likely Voters	51.5	48.5	0.0	3.0
		Actual	**52.5**	**47.0**	**0.5**	**5.5**
		2-Pty Vote	**52.8**	**47.2**	**—**	**5.5**
1950	Oct 30-Nov 3	Likely Voters	51.0	49.0	0.0	2.0
		Actual	**49.0**	**49.0**	**2.0**	**0.0**
		2-Pty Vote	**50.0**	**50.0**	**—**	**0.0**

Gallup Poll Sampling Procedures

Gallup Poll surveys conducted from 1935 through 1984 were based on personal in-home, face-to-face interviews. From 1985 through 1988, although a few surveys were based on telephone interviews, the majority was based on personal interviews. From 1989 to the present, virtually all Gallup Poll surveys are based on telephone interviews.

The majority of the findings reported in Gallup Poll surveys is based on samples consisting of a minimum of 1,000 interviews. The total number, however, may exceed 1,000, or even 1,500, interviews, where the survey specifications call for reporting the responses of low-incidence population groups such as young public-school parents or Hispanics.

Design of the Sample for Telephone Surveys

The findings from the telephone surveys are based on Gallup's standard national telephone samples, consisting of unclustered directory-assisted, random-digit telephone samples utilizing a proportionate, stratified sampling design. The random-digit aspect of the sample is used to avoid "listing" bias. Numerous studies have shown that households with unlisted telephone numbers are different from listed households. "Unlistedness" is due to household mobility or to customer requests to prevent publication of the telephone number. To avoid this source of bias, a random-digit procedure designed to provide representation of both listed and unlisted (including not-yet-listed) numbers is used. Since January 2008, cell phones have been included in the sample.

Telephone numbers for the continental United States are stratified into four regions of the country. The sample of telephone numbers produced by the described method is representative of all telephone households within the continental United States.

Only working banks of telephone numbers are selected. Eliminating nonworking banks from the sample increases the likelihood that any sampled telephone number will be associated with a residence.

Within each contacted household, an interview is sought with the adult 18 years of age or older living in the household who has had the most recent birthday (this is a method commonly employed to make a random selection within households without having to ask the respondent to provide a complete roster of adults living in the household). In the event that the sample becomes disproportionately female (due to higher cooperation rates typically observed for female respondents), the household selection criteria are adjusted to select only the male in the household who has had the most recent birthday (except in households where the adults are exclusively female).

A minimum of three calls (and up to six calls) is attempted to each selected telephone number to complete an interview. Time of day and the day of the week for callbacks are varied to maximize the chances of finding a respondent at home. All interviews are conducted on weekends or weekday evenings in order to contact potential respondents among the working population.

The final sample is weighted so that the distribution of the sample matches current estimates derived from the U.S. Census Bureau's Current Population Survey (CPS) for the adult population living in telephone households in the continental United States.

Weighting Procedures

After the survey data have been collected and processed, each respondent is assigned a weight so that the demographic characteristics of the total weighted sample of respondents match the latest estimates of the demographic characteristics of the adult population available from the U.S. Census Bureau. Gallup weights data to census estimates for gender, race, age, educational attainment, and region. Telephone surveys are weighted to match the characteristics of the adult population living in households with access to a telephone.

The procedures described above are designed to produce samples approximating the adult civilian population (18 and older) living in private households (that is, excluding those in prisons, hospitals, hotels, religious and educational institutions, and those living on reservations or military bases)—and in the case of telephone surveys, households with access to a telephone. Survey percentages may be applied to census estimates of the size of these populations to project percentages into numbers of people. The manner in which the sample is drawn also produces a sample that approximates the distribution of private households in the United States. Therefore, survey results also can be projected to numbers of households.

Sampling Tolerances

In interpreting survey results, it should be borne in mind that all sample surveys are subject to sampling error—that is, the extent to which the results may differ from what would be obtained if the whole population surveyed had been interviewed. The size of such sampling errors depends largely on the number of interviews.

The following tables may be used in estimating the sampling error of any percentage. The computed allowances have taken into account the effect of the sample design upon sampling error. They may be interpreted as indicating the range (plus or minus the figure shown) within which the results of repeated samplings in the same time period could be expected to vary, 95 percent of the time, assuming the same sampling procedure, the same interviewers, and the same questionnaire.

Table A shows how much allowance should be made for the sampling error of a percentage. Let us say a reported percentage is 33 for a group that includes 1,000 respondents. First, we go to the row headed "Percentages near 30" and then go across to the column headed "1,000." The number here is 3, which means that the 33 percent obtained in the sample is subject to a sampling error of plus or minus 3 points. Another way of saying it is that very probably (98 chances out of 100) the average of repeated samplings would be somewhere between 29 and 37, with the most likely figure being the 33 obtained.

In comparing survey results in two samples, such as for men and women, the question arises as to how large must a difference between them be before one can be reasonably sure that it reflects a real difference. In Tables B and C, the number of points that must be allowed for in such comparisons is indicated. Table B is for percentages near 20 or 80, and Table C is for percentages near 50. For percentages in between, the error to be allowed for is between those shown in the two tables.

Here is an example of how the tables would be used: Let us say that 50 percent of men respond a certain way and 40 percent of women also respond that way, for a difference of 10 percentage points between them. Can we say with any assurance that the 10-point difference reflects a real difference between men and women on the question? The sample contains approximately 500 men and 500 women.

Since the percentages are near 50, we consult Table C, and since the two samples are about 600 persons each, we look for the number in the column

TABLE A. Recommended Allowance for Sampling Error of a Percentage in Percentage Points (at 95 in 100 confidence level)

	Sample Size				
	1,000	750	500	250	100
Percentages near 10	2	2	3	4	6
Percentages near 20	3	3	4	5	9
Percentages near 30	3	4	4	6	10
Percentages near 40	3	4	5	7	10
Percentages near 50	3	4	5	7	11
Percentages near 60	3	4	5	7	10
Percentages near 70	3	4	4	6	10
Percentages near 80	3	3	4	5	9
Percentages near 90	2	2	3	4	6

Note: Confidence level indicates that the chances are 95 in 100 that the sampling is not larger than the figures shown.

Table B. Recommended Allowance for Sampling Error of the Difference in Percentage Points (at 95 in 100 confidence level): Percentages near 20 or percentages near 80

Size of Sample	750	500	250
750	4		
500	5	5	
250	6	7	8

Note: Confidence level indicates that the chances are 95 in 100 that the sampling is not larger than the figures shown.

Table C. Recommended Allowance for Sampling Error of the Difference in Percentage Points (at 95 in 100 confidence level): Percentages near 50

Size of Sample	750	500	250
750	6		
500	6	7	
250	8	8	10

Note: Confidence level indicates that the chances are 95 in 100 that the sampling is not larger than the figures shown.

headed "500" that is also in the row designated "500." We find the number 7 here. This means that the allowance for error should be 7 points, and that in concluding that the percentage among men is somewhere between 3 and 17 points higher than the percentage among women, we should be wrong only about 5 percent of the time. In other words, we can conclude with considerable confidence that a difference exists in the direction observed and that it amounts to at least 3 percentage points.

If, in another case, men's responses amount to 22 percent and women's 24 percent, we consult Table B because these percentages are near 20. We look for the number in the column headed "500" that is also in the row designated "500" and see that the number is 5. Obviously, then, the 2-point difference is inconclusive.

INDEX

A

Aaron, Hank, 1999:256, **2000:**1,
   2001:83, **2007:**1, 261
Abbas, Mahmoud, 2005:69, 107
Abbott, Jim, 2002:340–41
ABC News, 2004:30
abortion
   age and, **2004:**170, **2006:**307
   Bush, George W., and, **1999:**66,
      2000:226, 242, 248, 258, 275,
      428, **2002:**92, **2003:**394–95,
      2004:140–41, 169–70, 329,
      383–84, 428, 471, 473–74,
      2005:3–4, 156, 176
   church and, **2004:**473–74
   concern for, **2004:**170, 428
   as Congressional election issue,
      2002:291
   conservatives and, **2007:**295
   consider yourself pro-choice or
      pro-life, **1998:**159, **1999:**186,
      2000:110, **2002:**204–5,
      2003:178, 391, 394
   Constitution and, **2006:**307
   Democratic Party and, **2003:**5,
      2004:141, **2007:**221
   Democrats in Congress and,
      2002:291
   demographics and [list], **2003:**19

election of 2000 and, **2004:**
      140–41
   election of 2004 and,
      2004:140–41, 169–71, 383–84,
      428, 473–74
   gender and, **2004:**170, **2005:**175,
      245–46, 443
   geographic region and, **2006:**307
   Gore and, **2000:**242, 248, 258,
      275
   homosexuality and, **2004:**202–3
   ideology and, **2004:**250, 473–74,
      2005:245–46, 260, 405–6,
      443–44
   important president and Congress
      deal with next year, **2003:**4
   independents and, **2004:**141
   as issue to be addressed by next
      president, **2000:**212
   Kerry, John, and, **2004:**140–41,
      329, 383–84, 428, 471, 473–74
   legal issues in, opinions on,
      1998:159, **1999:**186,
      2000:110–12, **2002:**20, 204,
      2003:19–20, 178–80, 391,
      394
   liberals and, **2007:**295
   marriage amendment and,
      2004:202–3
   marriage and, **2006:**307

1

abortion *(continued)*

moderates and, **2007:**295

morality of, **2002:**149, 205, **2003:**159, 178–79, 218, **2004:**249–50

as most important issue, **1998:** 60–61, **1999:**195, **2001:**59, 121, 256, **2002:**10, 71, 116, 233, 360, **2003:**25, 62, 86, 122, 443, **2005:**3–4, 38, 99, 175, 213, **2006:**138–39, 288, 338, 479

as most important issue facing nation 25 years from now, **2002:**117

as murder, **1998:**157

"partial birth," **1998:**157, **2000:**112, 200, **2003:**391, 394

policies concerning, **2004:**130, 140–41, 169–71

satisfaction with, **2001:**29, **2002:**19–20

political affiliation and, **2005:**3–4, 175, 192–93, 245–46, 405, 443–44, **2007:**221

political ideology and, **2007:**295

in predictions for 2007, **2007:**1–2

as presidential election issue, **1999:**69, **2000:**19, 72, 192, 243, 281, **2003:**416

religion and, **2005:**125, 131–32, 150–51

Republican Party and, **2003:**5, **2004:**141, **2007:**221, 295

Republicans in Congress and, **2002:**291

rights movement

agree with goals of, **2000:**119

impact of, **2000:**119

Roe v. Wade was good thing for the country, **2003:**20

RU-486

heard or read about, **2000:**111

make available in U.S., **2000:**111

support for, **2003:**19–20, **2004:**169–71, 473–74

Supreme Court and, **2002:**205, **2004:**169

teenagers and, **2006:**307

voters, swing, and, **2004:**421

and voting, **1999:**186

Abramoff, Jack, 2006:4–5, 13–15, 226, 364

Academy Awards, 2000:98, **2001:**72–73, **2002:**79

like to see [list] win Oscar for Best Picture, **1998:**174–75, **1999:**254, **2000:**98

See also movies

accountants

can be trusted, **2002:**199

honesty and ethical standards of, **2000:**388, **2001:**265, **2002:**50, 373

accounting, 2004:271–72, **2005:**311, 422, 448

overall view of, **2001:**200, **2002:**240, **2003:**289

accuracy, viii, x–xi

See also individual polls

AC/DC, 2000:265

acid rain, 2004:141, 161, **2006:**165–66

worry about, **2000:**316, **2001:**90, **2002:**77, 113

actress

recommend as career for young woman, **1998:**239, **2001:**109

Adams, John, 2004:124

Adams, John Quincy, 2004:124

admiration, 2004:230, 233, 320–22, 351–52, 513–14, **2006:**536–37, **2007:**544–46

See also image

adultery, 2006:212–13, 218

adults

think few black people dislike whites, **2003:**220

advertising and public relations,
2004:260, 345–47, 360–61, 417,
444, 485, **2005:**311, 422, 448,
2006:341–42, 440, 463, 520
and children, **1998:**189
overall view of, **2001:**201,
2002:240, **2003:**289
practitioners of
honesty and ethical standards
of, **1999:**148, **2000:**389,
2001:265, **2002:**50, 373,
2003:422
Aerosmith, 2000:265
affirmative action, 2005:287–88,
314–15, 338
applicants to college should be
admitted on merit or background considered, **2003:**213
favor programs for racial minorities, **2003:**213
who has better chance of being
accepted to college, a black or
white equally qualified student,
2003:213
affluence, 2004:315
Afghanistan, 2001:239, **2004:**73,
2005:71, 78–79, 128–29, **2006:**72,
77, 79–80, 130–31, **2007:**78–81,
274, 340–41, 349, 542
as America's greatest enemy
today, **2001:**84
Clinton and, **1998:**204
opinion of, **2001:**233, **2002:**52,
2003:56
U.S. military action in,
1998:201–2, 204, **2001:**253,
2002:261, 301
accomplishments of, **2002:**24,
68, 194
and budget deficit, **2002:**22
effects of, **1998:**201
as mistake, **2002:**10, **2003:**240
timing of, **1998:**201
withdrawal from, **2002:**183

Africa
what happens in, as important to
U.S., **2000:**186
Agassi, Andre, 2001:142
age
abortion and, **2004:**170, **2006:**307
alcohol and, **2005:**261–62,
270–71
animal testing and, **2004:**215–16
approval ratings by, **2004:**184–85,
205–6, **2005:**145, 330,
2006:215, 316, 530
Bible and, **2006:**210,
2007:230–31
Bush, George W., and,
2004:137–38, 184–85, 205,
379, 442–43, **2005:**156,
2006:215, 316, 530
caretaker role and, **2005:**308
CBS News National Guard story
and, **2004:**394
Christmas and, **2004:**460,
2005:435, 478, **2006:**509
church and, **2004:**303–4, 512,
2005:114
civil liberties and, **2004:**19
Clinton, Bill, and, **2004:**205
Clinton, Hillary, and, **2005:**81,
2007:47, 124–25, 227–29,
253–54, 419, 423–24, 471–72,
547
Congress and, **2004:**205–6,
2005:145, 330, **2007:**91
conservatives and, **2004:**103
creationism and, **2004:**463,
2006:100, 231
credit cards and, **2004:**203–4
crime and, **2004:**478–79,
2005:413–14, 438, **2006:**490,
2007:47
Dean, Howard, and, **2004:**30
death penalty and, **2004:**454, 495,
2005:186, 457
debt and, **2005:**209

age *(continued)*
  diet and, **2004:**294
  divorce and, **2004:**131–32,
    2006:218
  drugs and, **2005:**407
  economy and, **2004:**205, **2005:**66,
    108, 470, **2007:**47
  education and, **2005:**66, 156
  Edwards, John, and, **2007:**47,
    124, 227–29, 419
  election of 2004 and, **2004:**22, 30,
    379, 408, 418, 423–24, 442–43
  employment and, **2004:**345,
    2005:135, 287, 290–92, 308,
    2006:177–78, 363, **2007:**378
  energy and, **2004:**121, **2005:**156,
    470, **2007:**47
  entertainment and, **2004:**61–62,
    88–89
  entrepreneurship and, **2005:**135
  environment and, **2004:**121, 160,
    2007:47, 127
  euthanasia and, **2005:**179
  evolution and, **2004:**464,
    2006:100, 231
  family size and, **2004:**128
  finances and, **2004:**175, 204, 207,
    234, **2005:**93–94, 209
  foreign affairs and, **2006:**71, 78,
    2007:47
  friendship and, **2004:**99–100
  gambling and, **2004:**123
  gasoline and, **2004:**234,
    2005:196, 470
  Gingrich, Newt, and, **2007:**187
  government and, **2004:**278
  guns and, **2005:**140, 438–39
  happiness and, **2004:**1–2
  health and, **2004:**468, 476–77
  healthcare and, **2004:**177, 477,
    2005:66, 156, 442, 454, 470,
    2007:47, 91, 182–83, 533
  health insurance and, **2004:**481,
    2005:13

homosexuality and, **2004:**62, 405,
    2005:142, **2007:**232
immigration and, **2005:**156, 470
income and, **2004:**203–4,
    2005:209
Internet and, **2004:**22, 108–9, 503,
    2006:11, 49, 55
investors and, **2004:**78–79
Iraq war and, **2004:**400, **2005:**66,
    145, 156, 244, 470, **2006:**403
Kerry, John, and, **2004:**30, 379,
    442–43
labor unions and, **2005:**323
law enforcement and, **2005:**420
lawsuits and, **2005:**66
liberals and, **2004:**103
life, satisfaction with, and,
    2004:72
love and, **2004:**62–63
manufactured goods and,
    2007:456
marriage and, **2004:**86–87,
    131–32, 223, 405, **2005:**66,
    142
Medicaid and, **2005:**13
Medicare and, **2004:**38, 109–10,
    137–38, **2005:**13
Middle East and, **2006:**123
military and, **2005:**218, **2006:**403
money and, **2005:**162
morality and, **2004:**214–316,
    2005:92, **2007:**47, 239
most important issues by,
    2005:470
movies and, **2004:**88–89,
    2005:60, **2006:**535
Nader, Ralph, and, **2004:**87
national defense and, **2007:**391
news and, **2005:**369
newspapers and, **2004:**503
news sources and, **2004:**503
nuclear weapons and, **2005:**292
Obama, Barack, and, **2007:**47,
    124, 227–29, 419, 462–63, 547

oil and, **2005:**470

opportunities and, **2004:**278,
  2005:287

patriotism and, **2005:**267

personal lives and, **2006:**143

pets and, **2006:**533, **2007:**518

political affiliation and, **2005:**265

president and, **2007:**77–78, 91

priorities and, **2007:**91

profanity and, **2004:**62

Protestantism and, **2004:**511

race and, **2004:**19, 223

radio and, **2004:**503

reading and, **2005:**203

religion and, **2004:**120, 511–12,
  2005:133, 234, 447, **2006:**196,
  210, 259, 334, 493,
  2007:230–31

retirement and, **2004:**175, 207,
  209, 465–66

satisfaction with U.S. and,
  2004:205, **2006:**81–82, 238

savings and, **2005:**209, **2006:**261

school performance and,
  2004:67–68

seasons and, **2005:**223

September 11, 2001, terrorist
  attacks and, **2007:**395

sex and, **2004:**61–62

smoking and, **2004:**79–80, 307,
  2005:303

Social Security and, **2004:**109–10,
  2005:5, 36, 64, 66, 77–78, 156,
  165–66, 239–40, 470,
  2006:261

spending and, **2004:**460,
  2005:209, 435

sports and, **2004:**43–44, **2005:**54

standard of living and,
  2004:176–77

stress and, **2004:**181–82, **2007:**35

suicide and, **2005:**179

taxes and, **2007:**47

television and, **2004:**61–62, 503

terrorism and, **2005:**66, 470,
  2006:373, **2007:**47

time and, **2004:**181, **2005:**225

traditional values and, **2004:**57

vacation and, **2005:**474–75

Valentine's Day and, **2004:**63

violence and, **2004:**61–62

weight and, **2004:**331–32,
  2005:296, 305

World War II and, **2004:**228,
  2005:292

See also children; elderly;
  teenagers

aging

as biggest challenge you face
  today, **2000:**192

agnosticism, 2004:118, 252–53, 255,
  358–59, 511

agriculture, 2005:311–12, 356–57,
  422

support use of biotechnology in,
  1999:226

as worst problem facing your
  community, **2000:**191

AIDS (Acquired Immune Deficiency Syndrome), 2004:458,
  490, **2005:**72, 431–32,
  2006:481–82, 521

cured by year 2025, **1998:**222

as most important issue,
  1998:60–61, **1999:**195–96,
  2001:59, 121, 256, **2002:**10,
  71, 116, 360, **2003:**25, 62, 87

as most important issue facing
  nation 25 years from now,
  2002:117

worried you will experience this
  illness, **2003:**424

Aikman, Troy, 2000:289

air, 2004:141, 160–61

air conditioning

any, where you live, **1999:**217

aircraft, combat

approve of women flying, **2002:**3

Air Force, 2002:152, **2004:**220–21
airline industry
overall view of, **2001:**201,
2002:240, **2003:**289
passengers
enjoy flying today more than in
past, **1999:**139
ever felt rage at airlines or airline employees when flying,
1999:140
satisfaction with, **1999:**139,
2000:292
satisfaction with job airlines
are doing, **1999:**139
taken how many trips on com-
mercial airliner in past
twelve months, **1999:**139,
2000:51, 292
safety in
avoid traveling on January 1 to
protect yourself against Y2K
problems, **1999:**157, 246
confidence in airline companies that fly across country,
1999:146, **2000:**38
confidence in airline companies that fly internationally,
1999:146, **2000:**38
confidence in air traffic con-
trollers, **1999:**147, **2000:**38
confidence in companies that
manufacture airplanes,
1999:147, **2000:**38
confidence in federal agencies,
1999:146, **2000:**38
confidence in flying on airlines
today, **2000:**52
confidence in ground mainte-
nance crews, **1999:**146,
2000:38
confidence in pilots, **1999:**147,
2000:38
confidence in regional and
commuter airlines,
1999:146, **2000:**38

confident about safety standards of major airlines,
1999:147, **2000:**38–39, 52
ever frightened when you fly,
1999:146
less likely to fly as result of
Alaska Airlines crash,
2000:52
less likely to fly as result of
EgyptAir crash, **1999:**147
likely that air traffic control
systems will fail as result of
Y2K problems,
1999:157–58, 247
security in
federal government responsibility will make airport
security better, **2002:**41
how difficult for terrorist to
smuggle deadly weapon
onto airplane, **2002:**41
how difficult for terrorist to
smuggle explosives onto
airplane, **2002:**41–42
how much has security been
improved at airports since
September 11 attacks,
2002:41
very afraid to fly tomorrow,
2002:41
stewardess, recommend as career
for young woman, **1998:**239,
2001:109
strikes in
Bush should use his emergency
powers to prevent, **2001:**85
would be major inconvenience
to you, **2001:**85
would favor airline workers or
airlines in event of, **2001:**85
travel on
before attacks of 9/11 were
you considering flying
somewhere for the holidays,
2001:254

events of 9/11 make it less
likely you will fly some-
where for the holidays,
2001:254
events of 9/11 make you less
willing to fly, **2001:**254
have done or considered avoid-
ing since terrorist attacks,
2001:242
airplanes, 2005:140, 273, 311, 422
fear of flying, **1998:**238
air pollution
worry about, **2001:**90
airport security
Gallup analysis of, **2001:**245
Alabama, 2002:160
Alaska, 2002:160
**Alaskan Arctic National Wildlife
Refuge**
favor opening up for oil explo-
ration, **2001:**68, 100, 118–19,
258
Albright, Madeleine, 1998:2, 154,
1999:242, **2000:**175, 431,
2001:278, **2002:**400, **2003:**455,
2004:514, **2005:**116
opinion of, **1998:**155, 253,
1999:45, **2000:**211
**alcohol, alcoholic beverages,
1999:**279–80, **2000:**400–401,
2001:200, **2002:**228, **2003:**275,
329, **2004:**294, **2005:**260–62,
270–72, 431
as cause of trouble in your family,
1999:280, **2000:**401,
2002:229, **2003:**330–31
cheating and, **2004:**192
versus cigarettes, creates most
problems for society, **1999:**
280
drink more than you should,
1999:280, **2000:**401,
2002:228, **2003:**330
existentialism and, **2004:**47–48
families and, **2004:**123

favor federal law to lower drinking
age to 18 in all states, **2001:**200
health and, **2004:**476, 483
people who drink vs. non-
drinkers, **2002:**5
how many drinks in past seven
days, **1999:**280, **2000:**401,
2002:228, **2003:**330
how often do you drink alcoholic
beverages, **2002:**5
last had alcoholic drink,
2002:228, **2003:**329–30
made serious effort to stop drinking, **1999:**280, **2000:**401
in moderation, good for your
health, **2001:**200, **2003:**331
most often drink liquor, wine, or
beer, **2002:**228, **2003:**330
penalties for underage drinking
should be made more strict,
2001:200
as problem, **2004:**123, 182–83
respect you have for person who
drinks alcohol, **2003:**275
teenagers and, **2004:**47–48,
182–83, 270–71
See also drugs
alcohol abuse
as worst problem facing your
community, **2000:**190, 192
alcoholism
has increased in Eastern Europe,
1999:231
need to know if presidential candidate were an alcoholic,
1998:36–37
Alexander, Lamar
likely to support, **1998:**65, 227,
1999:71
opinion of, **1998:**64, **1999:**46
alienation, 2004:47–48
aliens (extraterrestrials)
believe in, **2001:**137
humans will have made contact
with, by year 2025, **1998:**221

aliens (extraterrestrials) *(continued)*
likely to be friendly by year 2025,
1998:221
See also immigrants
Alito, Samuel, 2007:417, 427
Allard, Wayne, 2002:340
Allawi, Iyad, 2004:262–63
Allen, Curtis, 2004:426
Allen, George, 2005:300, 310, 468,
2006:66–67, 235–36, 417, 463,
477, 531, **2007:**22, 68
Allen, Steve, 2002:146
Allen, Thad, 2005:337
allies, 2005:71–73
"Ally McBeal," 1998:61–62
al-Majid, Ali Hassan, 2004:209
al-Qaeda, 2002:285–86, 302,
2003:49, 52, 59, 199, **2004:**53,
134–35, 146–47, 167–68, 287
alternative fuels, 2006:114–15,
128
al-Zawahiri, Ayman, 2007:199
Alzheimer's disease, 2004:232
worried you will experience this
illness, **2003:**424
**American Academy of Pediatrics,
2004:**385
**American Association of Retired
Persons (AARP), 2004:**223
**American Automobile Association,
2004:**130
American Beauty **(movie), 2000:**98
**American Civil Liberties Union,
2004:**94
**American Diploma Project,
2004:**67–68
**American Medical Association,
2004:**417, **2005:**442–43
American people, 2005:359–60, 378
American consumers are to blame
for country's energy problems,
2001:131
American royal family good thing
for people of this country,
2002:163

can retain their lifestyle and the
current energy problems can be
solved, **2001:**131
consider yourself a feminist,
2001:152
Democrats or Republicans in Congress would do better job deal-
ing with problems of,
2002:171
describe your mood today,
2001:270
economic conditions in country
right now getting better or
worse, **2003:**63
economic conditions in this country today, **2003:**62–63
experience stress in your daily
life, **2002:**1–2
fears of [list], **2001:**70
free to control their own lives and
futures, **2002:**59
gap between rich and poor
as most important issue,
2001:58, 121, 255, **2002:**9,
70, 116, 232, 359
as most important issue facing
nation 25 years from now,
2002:117
how many hours of sleep do you
get a night, **2001:**271
how much do the American people do to protect the environment, **2001:**100
how much time to relax each day
[list], **2002:**347–48
how often you experience stress in
your daily life, **2001:**271
important immigrants learn to
speak English, **2001:**89
important president and Congress
deal with problems of next
year, **2002:**171
most important issue facing this
country today [list],
2003:61–62

and patriotism, **2000:**378

personally speak language other than English well enough to hold a conversation, **2001:**89

prefer to have job outside the home, **2001:**152

racial minorities have equal job opportunities, **2001:**147, 152

rating personal life, **2002:**25–26

rating state of the nation, **2002:**25

satisfaction with

community as place to live, **2001:**146

current housing, **2001:**146

education, **2001:**146

family life, **2001:**146

financial situation, **2001:**146

job, **2001:**147

opportunities to succeed in life, **2001:**147

safety from physical harm or violence, **2001:**147

way things are going in U.S., **2002:**208, **2003:**61

way things are going in your personal life, **2001:**270

way things going in your local community, **2001:**26

way things going in your state, **2001:**26

time enough today to do what you want, **2002:**1

trust in, **2004:**164

making judgments about issues facing our country, **2002:**282

which foreign language do you speak (asked of foreign-speaking people), **2001:**89

women have equal job opportunities with men, **2001:**152

would personally commit yourself in service to your neighbors and the nation, **2002:**30

"America's Funniest Home Videos," 1998:61–62

Anaheim Angels, 2001:82

Anderson, John, 2004:349

Andrews, V. C., 1999:267

Angelou, Maya, 1998:2, 154, **1999:**242, **2000:**431, **2002:**400, **2003:**455, **2004:**514, **2005:**483, **2006:**536

animals, 2004:147, 215–16, 249–50

cloning of, as morally acceptable, **2003:**159, 179, 218

deserve exact same rights as people, **2003:**169

fur of, buying and wearing clothing made of, as morally acceptable, **2002:**149, **2003:**159, 178, 218, **2004:**215, 250

medical testing on, as morally acceptable, **2002:**149, **2003:**159, 178, 218

rights movement

agree with goals of, **2000:**120

impact of, **2000:**119

support banning all types of hunting, **2003:**170

support banning medical research on animals, **2003:**170

support banning product testing on animals, **2003:**170

support passing strict laws concerning treatment of farm animals, **2003:**170

worry about extinction of, **2002:**76, 81, 114

worry about loss of habitat for, **2001:**90

Annan, Kofi, 1998:33, **2002:**295, 400, **2003:**454, **2006:**536

anthrax, 2001:237–38, 242, 250–51, 262, **2002:**299

antique restoration

hobby you are particularly interested in, **2002:**7

anti-war activity, 2004:77

AOL (America Online)

merger with Time Warner, as good or bad, **2000:**42

apathy

as worst problem facing your community, **2000:**191

approval ratings

by age, **2004:**184–85, 205–6, **2005:**145, 330, **2006:**215, 316, 530

blacks and, **2004:**184–85

in blue states, **2004:**184

of Bush, Barbara, **2006:**53

of Bush, George H. W., **2004:**7–8, 17, 113, 124, 151, 211–12, 229–32, 258–59, 265, 303, 414, 416, 422, 444, **2005:**26, 33–34, 48–51, 118, 417, **2006:**6, 40–41, 96, 170, 182, 190, 200–201, 245–46, 329, 466, 539, **2007:**26, 100, 313

of Bush, George W., **2004:**6–8, 12, 16–18, 20, 48–50, 52–53, 58–61, 64, 68, 75–76, 95–96, 104–5, 112–13, 121, 124, 133–35, 137–39, 145, 151, 162–63, 166–68, 184–85, 187–89, 191, 193, 196–97, 205, 210–12, 217–18, 222, 229–30, 235–36, 240–42, 257–60, 265–67, 282, 284, 297–98, 302–3, 335, 342, 346, 354, 357–58, 389, 391, 397, 405–6, 413–14, 416, 418, 421–23, 430, 437, 444, 450, 452, 504, **2005:**11–12, 15–16, 18–20, 24–31, 33–34, 38–39, 41, 48–52, 59–60, 62–64, 68–69, 87–90, 98–99, 102–3, 111–14, 118–20, 130–31, 141–42, 155–57, 164–67, 169, 173, 193–94, 212, 214, 227, 236, 239, 242–43, 252, 262–64, 273, 278, 280–81,

296–97, 317–18, 320–21, 325–26, 337, 342, 345–46, 351–53, 359, 375, 384, 391–93, 397, 402, 417–18, 424–26, 428, 433–34, 445, 451, 461–62, 464, 471, **2006:**5–7, 23–24, 29, 40–43, 46, 53–54, 61, 91–93, 95–98, 105, 116–17, 120–21, 139–40, 154–56, 169–72, 174, 181–83, 186–90, 193, 196–97, 200–201, 214–15, 240–41, 243–44, 262–63, 276, 302–4, 309, 315–16, 328–29, 347–48, 352–53, 374–75, 382–83, 387, 398, 404, 421–22, 433–34, 443, 465–66, 468, 476, 515–16, 518, 530–31, 539, **2007:**13–14, 25–26, 52–53, 65–66, 86–87, 100, 115–16, 152, 166–67, 200–202, 210–11, 224–25, 270–72, 280–81, 297–99, 312–13, 359, 365–67, 400, 408–9, 413, 415, 418, 439–40, 480–82, 484–86, 501–2, 529

of Carter, Jimmy, **2004:**8, 17, 151, 211–12, 229, 231–32, 259, 265, 303, 414, 416, 444, **2005:**26, 50–51, 118, 417, **2006:**40–41, 53, 169–70, 182, 190, 245–46, 329, 466, 539, **2007:**25, 100, 313, 484

of Clinton, Bill, **2004:**8, 17, 104, 113, 151, 205, 211–12, 229–32, 247–49, 258–59, 265–66, 303, 413–14, 416, 422, 444, 450, **2005:**24–27, 33–34, 49–51, 118–19, 141, 263, 320, 392–93, 397, **2006:**23–24, 40–42, 53, 92, 96, 172, 182, 190, 200–201, 245–46, 329, 375, 434, 466, 539, **2007:**25–26, 166, 313, 484

of Congress, **2004:**68–69, 205–6,
450–51, **2005:**98, 144–45,
169–70, 212–14, 330, 384–85,
396–97, 412, 430, **2007:**38–39,
53, 118–19, 153, 201–2,
210–11, 266–67, 271–72,
322–23, 364–65, 384–85,
408–9, 418, 441–42, 494–95,
501–2, 529
of Democratic Party, **2004:**68–69,
184–85, 205, 211–12, 229–30,
235, 282, 422, 450–51, 504,
2005:412, 430, **2007:**14, 39,
53, 66–67, 100, 118–19,
152–53, 200–202, 210–12,
224–25, 249, 267, 297–99,
322–23, 364–67, 380, 400,
408, 417, 440–42, 484–85,
502
economy and, **2004:**6–7, 49, 58,
64, 139, 187–88, 191, 230–31,
236, 257–59, 389, 450, 452,
2006:54, 92, 116–17, 154–56,
187, 200–201, 243–44, 303,
348, 422
education and, **2004:**7, 184–85,
2005:15–16, 19, 27, 144,
2006:215
of Eisenhower, Dwight D.,
2004:8, 17, 151, 229, 231, 259,
265–66, 303, 413–14, 416,
444, 450, **2007:**25–26, 166,
313
elections and, **2004:**211–12, 231,
265–66, 302–3, 342, 357–58,
405–6, 413–14, 416, 430, 444,
450, **2006:**119–20, 171–72,
174–75, 466, 468–69
energy and, **2004:**139, 235,
2005:27, 102–3, **2006:**54,
116–17, 154–56, 169–71,
186–87, 243–44, 348
environment and, **2004:**139,
2005:15–16, 19, 27

federal budget and, **2005:**15–16,
19, 27, 68, 425
finances and, **2007:**486
of Ford, Gerald, **2004:**8, 17,
211–12, 229, 231–32, 259,
265, 414, 444, **2005:**26, 118,
2007:313, 484
foreign affairs and, **2004:**6–7, 49,
188, 389, 450, **2006:**54, 187,
200–201, 243–44, 303, 348
gasoline and, **2004:**222,
2005:169, 325, 346
by gender, **2004:**184–85,
2005:145, **2006:**53, 215, 316,
348, 530
by geographic region, **2006:**215,
316, 530
of Gonzales, Alberto, **2007:**172
of Gore, Al, **2006:**95–96
healthcare and, **2004:**7, 49–50,
450, **2005:**15–16, 19, 27, 325
of Hoover, Herbert, **2004:**413–14
Hurricane Katrina and, **2005:**337,
345–46, 351, **2006:**348
ideology and, **2004:**184–85,
2005:144–45, 417
immigration and, **2005:**15–16, 19,
425, 451
income and, **2004:**184–85,
2005:144, **2006:**215
independents and, **2004:**184–85,
211–12, 229–30, 235, 422,
450, 504, **2007:**14, 39, 53,
66–67, 100, 118–19, 152–53,
200, 202, 210–12, 224–25,
249, 267, 297–99, 322–23,
364–67, 380, 400, 408, 417,
440–42, 484–85, 502
Iran-Contra affair and,
2004:230–31
Iraq war and, **2004:**17, 49,
166, 188, 197, 240–42, 258,
260, 267, 335, 389, 450,
2005:11–12, 15–16, 19, 27,

approval ratings *(continued)*
> 41, 59–60, 88, 90, 111–12,
> 131, 167, 194, 236, 242,
> 317–18, 325–26, 346, 351,
> 353, 359, 425, 428, 445,
> 461–62, 464, 471, **2006:**46, 54,
> 92, 154–56, 187, 240–41,
> 243–44, 303, 348, 422
> Israeli/Palestinian conflict and,
> **2004:**389
> of Johnson, Lyndon, **2004:**8, 17,
> 151, 229–32, 240–41, 259,
> 265–66, 444, 450, **2007:**25–26,
> 313, 484
> of Kennedy, John F., **2004:**17,
> 151, 231–32, 303, **2005:**26,
> 118, **2007:**313
> of labor unions, **2007:**380
> Medicare and, **2004:**137–38
> Middle East and, **2006:**303, 348
> of Nixon, Pat, **2006:**52
> of Nixon, Richard, **2004:**8, 17,
> 151, 211–12, 229–32, 240, 259,
> 265–66, 303, 413–14, 416, 444,
> 450, **2005:**24–27, 118–19, 141,
> 263, 320, 392–93, 417,
> **2006:**23–24, 92, 96, 169–70,
> 182, 245–46, 329, 375, 434,
> 466, 539, **2007:**25–26, 100,
> 312–13, 400, 484
> party identification and, **2006:**29
> political affiliation and, **2005:**69,
> 120, 141–42, 144, 168–69,
> 214, 320, 330, 346, 391–92,
> 397–98, 412, 417, 426, 430,
> 433, 461–62, **2006:**5, 24–25,
> 46, 51–54, 94–96, 104–5,
> 120–21, 154–56, 172, 183,
> 189–90, 193, 197, 214–15,
> 241, 244, 246, 262–63,
> 272–73, 303, 316, 348,
> 374–75, 421, 515–16, 527–28,
> 530, **2007:**14, 39, 53, 66–67,
> 100, 118–19, 152–53,

> 200–202, 210–12, 224–25,
> 249, 267, 297–99, 322–23,
> 364–67, 380, 400, 408, 417,
> 440–42, 484–85, 502
> prosperity and, **2004:**139
> of Quayle, Dan, **2006:**95–96
> race and, **2004:**184–85, **2005:**145,
> 263–64, 342, **2006:**215, 276,
> 530
> of Reagan, Nancy, **2006:**52
> of Reagan, Ronald, **2004:**8, 17,
> 151, 211–12, 229–32, 259,
> 265–66, 303, 413–14, 416, 444,
> 450, **2006:**7, 23–24, 40–41, 92,
> 182, 190, 200–201, 245–46,
> 329, 375, 434, 466, 539,
> **2007:**25–26, 166, 313, 484
> in red states, **2004:**184
> religion and, **2004:**217–18
> of Republican Party, **2004:**68–69,
> 184, 205, 211–12, 229–30,
> 235, 282, 422, 450–51, 504,
> **2005:**342, 412, 430, **2007:**14,
> 39, 53, 66–67, 100, 118–19,
> 152–53, 200–202, 210–12,
> 224–25, 249, 267, 297–99,
> 322–23, 364–67, 380, 400,
> 408, 417, 440–42, 484–85, 502
> by residential areas, **2006:**215
> retrospective, **2004:**232, 248–49
> of Roosevelt, Eleanor, **2006:**52
> of Roosevelt, Franklin D.,
> **2004:**450
> of Rumsfeld, Donald, **2004:**194,
> 503–4
> Schiavo, Terri and, **2005:**131
> September 11, 2001, terrorist
> attacks and, **2005:**26–27
> Social Security and, **2005:**15–16,
> 19, 27, 59–60, 62–64, 68,
> 87–89, 119–20, 130–31,
> 164–66, 194, 239
> of Supreme Court, **2006:**404
> in swing states, **2004:**184–85

taxes and, **2004:**7

terrorism and, **2004:**134–35, 167–68, 188, 197, 258–59, 267, 389, 450, **2006:**54, 92–93, 154–56, 187, 240–41, 243–44, 303, 309, 348, 422

of Truman, Harry, **2004:**17, 229, 231, 265, 437, 444, 450, **2005:**26–27, 118–19, 263, 320, 392–93, 417, **2007:**25–26, 100, 166, 312–13, 400

tsunami disaster and, **2005:**15

veterans and, **2004:**418

Vietnam War and, **2004:**240–41

whites and, **2004:**184

See also image

Arab nations, 1998:221, 240

See also Muslim nations; Palestinian Arabs

Arabs, 2007:353

living in U.S., have less trust in since September 11, **2002:**266, 276

opinion of, **2001:**233

See also Palestinian Arabs

Arafat, Yasser, 1998:155, **1999:**45, **2000:**210–11, 415, **2002:**48, 94, 161, 170

Archives of Pediatrics and Adolescent Medicine, **2004:**148

Arctic National Wildlife Refuge (ANWR), 2002:73, 121, **2003:**92, **2006:**128

Arizona, 2002:160

Arizona Diamondbacks, 2001:82

Arkansas, 2002:160, 339–40

armed forces. *See* Military, U.S.

Armey, Dick, 1999:47

Armstrong, Lance, 2000:289, **2001:**142

Army, 2002:152, **2004:**220–21, 505

art, 2004:296

hobby you are particularly interested in, **2002:**7

Artest, Ron, 2004:487–88

arthritis/rheumatoid arthritis

worried you will experience this illness, **2003:**424

Arthur Andersen, 2002:129

arts

immigrants and, **2001:**171, **2002:**226

As Good As It Gets **(movie), 1998:**175

Ashcroft, John, 1998:64–65, 227, **2001:**16, 254, 269, **2004:**94, 480–81

Asia

financial crisis in

impact on U.S. economy, **1998:**157–58

U.S. should help solve, **1998:**158

what happens in, as important to U.S., **2000:**186

Asian Americans, 2006:408–9, 494

Asians, 2004:274–76, **2005:**133, 254–55, 257, **2007:**337–39, 353

satisfied way they are treated, **2003:**360

Askew, Reubin, 2004:42

aspirations, 2004:263–65

astrology

believe in, **2001:**137

atheism, atheists, 2004:118, 252–53, 255, 358–59, 511

vote for atheist presidential nominee, **1999:**53

athletes

greatest active today [list], **2000:**289

greatest of century [list], **2000:**1

professional, can be trusted, **2002:**199

athletics. *See* sports

Atkins diet, 2004:294–95

Atlanta, 2000:298–99, **2001:**235, **2004:**448–49

Atlanta Braves, 2001:81

attentiveness

to CBS News National Guard
story, **2004:**393–94

to China production stories,
2007:377

of Democratic Party, **2004:**143,
313

to Diana, Princess, death of,
2005:8

to Dubai ports sale, **2006:**91

to elections, **2004:**142–43, 282,
297–99, 311, 313, 356–57,
407–8, 412, 438–40, **2005:**8,
2006:467–69

to foreign affairs, **2004:**101,
2006:57–58, 71

to government surveillance,
2006:15–16, 33–34, 65, 198

to Hurricane Katrina, **2005:**336

to Imus, Don, story, **2007:**169

of independents, **2004:**143, 313

to Iraq, **2004:**394, **2005:**8, 336,
467

to Iraq Study Group, **2006:**514

to Israel/Lebanon conflict,
2006:314

to Jackson, Michael, molestation
trial, **2005:**157, 219

to Libby story, **2006:**144,
2007:115

to media, **2007:**193

to Mohammed cartoons,
2006:58–59

to mortgage crisis, **2007:**391

to news stories, **2004:**393–94

to Persian Gulf War, **2005:**8

to Plame, Valerie, story, **2005:**277

of Republican Party, **2004:**143,
313

to Schiavo, Terri, **2005:**105

to school vouchers, **2004:**390

to September 11, 2001, terrorist
attacks, **2005:**8, 336, **2007:**115

to Simpson, O. J., murder trial,
2005:157, 219

to sniper shootings, **2005:**8

to State of the Union address,
2005:52, **2006:**41–42, 45

to stem cell research, **2005:**195

to Supreme Court, **2005:**328,
2006:32

to tsunami disaster, **2005:**8

to U.S. Department of Justice
story, **2007:**128, 171

See also familiarity

attorney

recommend as career for young
woman, **2001:**109

Attorney General

know name of, **2000:**34

Augustine, saint, 2004:227

Australia, 2001:35, 43, 84,
2004:73

automobile(s)

anyone in your household own a
sport utility vehicle, **2000:**80

car owned by you stolen,
2000:329

car owned by you vandalized,
2000:330

dealers

can be trusted, **2002:**199

rate honesty and ethical standards of, **2002:**373

favor setting higher emissions
standards for, **2002:**73

favor setting higher emission standards for, **2003:**93

less likely to buy large car or
sports utility vehicle due to gas
prices, **2000:**107

noticed rise in interest rates for
loans for, **2000:**185

ownership of, **2004:**440–41

racing, **2004:**43–45, 489,
2006:135, **2007:**24

fan of, **2001:**81

as favorite sport to watch,
1998:237, **2000:**136
replaced by mass transportation
by year 2025, **1998:**222
restoring
hobby you are particularly
interested in, **2002:**7
rising interest rates affected your
decision to buy, **2000:**80
and traffic problems, **1999:**259,
2000:177, 179–80, 190
automobile industry, 2005:311,
422, **2006:**114–15, 341–43, 520
mechanics, **2004:**484
honesty and ethical standards
of, **1999:**148, **2000:**389,
2001:265
overall view of, **2001:**201,
2002:240, **2003:**289
salesmen, **2004:**485
honesty and ethical standards
of, **2000:**389, **2001:**265,
2003:422–23

B

Babbitt, Bruce, 2004:43
babies. *See* children
Backlin, Jim, 2005:142
Badnarik, Michael, 2004:378–79
Baker, James, 2006:513–16
Bakker, Jim, 2004:251
Baldwin, Alec, 2003:80
ballots, 2004:167
See also voting
Baltic States, 1998:171
Baltimore Orioles, 2001:81
Baltimore Ravens, 2001:25
banker(s)
honesty and ethical standards
of, **1999:**148, **2000:**388,
2001:265, **2002:**373,
2003:422–23

recommend as career for young
man, **1998:**238
banks and banking, 2001:201,
2002:240, **2003:**289, **2004:**224,
306, 361, 407, 485, **2005:**201,
311, 422, 448–49, **2006:**233,
341–43, 519, **2007:**269–71,
385–87, 528–29
confidence in, **1998:**181,
1999:209, **2000:**209,
2001:149, **2002:**184,
2003:205–6
good for consumers when two
large banks merge, **1998:**176
mortgages, **2004:**185–87
Y2K computer problems and,
1999:157–58, 246
Baptists
vote for Baptist presidential nominee, **1999:**54
Barak, Ehud
know name (Barak) of prime minister of Israel, **2000:**34
opinion of, **2000:**210, 415
Barbour, Haley, 2005:468, **2006:**67
Bartlett, Dan, 2004:210, **2005:**315
baseball, 1998:226, **1999:**254,
256–57, **2000:**108, **2001:**80,
82–83, **2002:**95, 179, 218, 249–50,
2003:197–98, 245–46, 426,
2004:43–45, 144, 367, 487–89
annoyances in [list], **2002:**95
as favorite sport to watch,
1998:237, **2000:**135
as favorite Summer Olympic
event, **2000:**307
games too long, or not, **2002:**95
greatest player in game today
[list], **1998:**226
greatest player of all time [list],
1999:256
most like to get a ticket to World
Series, **2001:**24
stadiums, **1999:**266

Baseball Hall of Fame, **1999:**266,
  2007:261
basketball, 1998:226, **1999:**251–52,
  2001:24–25, 81, **2004:**43–45,
  144, 367–68, 487–89, **2006:**135,
  2007:24, 151
  fan of, **1998:**226, **1999:**251,
    2000:108, **2001:**81
  as favorite sport to watch,
    1998:237, **2000:**135
  as favorite Summer Olympic
    event, **2000:**307
bathing
  take a bath or shower in winter
    how often, **2000:**5
Bauer, Gary, 2005:354, **2007:**251
  likely to support, **1998:**65,
    1999:71, 99, 117–18,
    2000:7–8, 26, 28
  opinion of, **1998:**64, **1999:**46
  qualifications of, **2000:**35–36
Baumeister, Roy, 2004:48
**Bay Area Laboratory Co-Opera-
  tive (BALCO), 2004:**144
Bayh, Birch, 2004:42
Bayh, Evan, 2005:300, 468,
  2006:66, 477, 531, **2007:**21,
  67, 75
The Beach Boys, 2000:265
The Beatles, 2000:265
Beatty, Warren, 1999:84, 90
beautician
  recommend as career for young
    woman, **1998:**239, **2001:**109
A Beautiful Mind (movie), **2002:**79
The Bee Gees, 2000:265
beer, 2004:294
  See also alcohol
Benedict XVI, 2005:482–83,
  2006:536
Benton, Oliver, 2004:108–9
Bentsen, Lloyd, 2004:314
Berlin Wall, fall of, 2002:1989
  Germany better off since,

  1999:231, **2000:**4
  as most important event in twenti-
    eth century, **2002:**175
  Russia better off since, **1999:**231,
    2000:4
  U.S. better off since, **1999:**231,
    2000:4
Bernanke, Ben, 2004:425,
  2007:204–5, 391–92
Berry, Halle, 2002:79
biathlon
  as favorite Winter Olympic event,
    2002:36
Bible, 1998:187, 241–42, **2000:**200,
  349, **2004:**118–19, 462–63,
  2007:229–31, 431
Biden, Joe, 2001:192, **2005:**300,
  468, **2006:**66, 235–36, 477,
  501–2, 531
  gender and, **2007:**124
  likely to support, **2002:**90
  veterans and, **2007:**370
Bies, Susan Schmidt, 2005:180
bilingual education
  teach non-English-speaking stu-
    dents using immersion or,
    1998:70–71
**Bill Haley and the Comets,
  2000:**265
Bill of Rights
  as document guaranteeing free
    press, **2000:**141
bingo
  hobby you are particularly inter-
    ested in, **2002:**7
  played, for money, **1999:**264
bin Laden, Osama, 2004:53, 146, 363
  and anthrax, **2001:**238
  capabilities of, **2002:**262, 276,
    302, **2003:**313
  capture of
    follow-up to, **2001:**264, 273
    as goal, **2001:**271
    importance of, **2002:**44

as likely, **2001:**263, 272,
2002:68, 262, 301–2
strategies for, **2001:**253,
2002:24, **2003:**440
opinion of, **2001:**233
and September 11 terrorist
attacks, **2001:**264, 273
as threat, **2002:**285–86, 302
and U.S. success in Afghanistan,
2001:263, **2002:**24, 68, 194
See also al-Qaeda
biotechnology, 2004:394
bioterrorism, 2005:431–32,
2006:481–82
bird flu, 2005:431–32
birth control, 2005:125
birth defects
think that cigarette smoking is
cause of, **1999:**276
birth rate, 2004:490
Black History Month, 2004:66
blackouts, power, 2004:120, 122,
129, 148
blacks
abortion and, **2000:**281
approval ratings, **2001:**145, **2005:**
263–64, 342, **2006:**215, 276
budget surplus and, **2000:**281
Bush, George W., and,
2000:281–82, 424–25,
2004:184–85, **2005:**263–64,
341–44, 346, **2006:**215, 276,
297
church and, **2004:**303–4, 512,
2005:233
clothing and, **2005:**274
college acceptance and, **2003:**213
college and, **2006:**484
community and, **2004:**18–19, 282
cost of living and, **2006:**484
crime and, **2006:**279, **2007:**304, 316
death penalty and, **2004:**453–54
debt and, **2006:**484
defense and, **2000:**281

Democratic Party and, **2000:**282,
2004:318, 368, **2007:**277–78,
281
demographics of, **2001:**135
discrimination and, **2000:**282,
2001:147, **2003:**296–97,
2004:290–91
economy and, **2000:**280,
2004:276–78, **2007:**304, 316
education and, **2000:**281,
2004:18–19, 199–201, 276–77,
317–18, 377, 455–56,
2006:279–80, 290
election of 2000 and,
2000:424–26
election of 2004 and, **2004:**333
election of 2006 and, **2006:**253,
297–98, 378
employment and, **2004:**18–19,
276–77, 290, 350–51,
2005:286–87, 314,
2006:86–87, 279–81,
2007:287, 293–94, 304
energy and, **2005:**286, **2006:**484
entertainment and, **2004:**290–91
experiences of, **2003:**221
families and, **2004:**18–19
finances and, **2004:**18–19,
291–92, **2005:**93–94, 274
food and, **2005:**274, **2007:**304
friendship and, **2004:**282
gasoline and, **2005:**286,
2006:279, 484
Gore, Al, and, **2006:**321
government and, **2004:**278,
2005:341–44, 394, **2006:**279,
2007:179–80, 316
gun control and, **2000:**281
happiness of, **2007:**554
health and, **2004:**18–19, 291
healthcare and, **2000:**281,
2004:290–91, 304–5,
2005:136, **2006:**279, 484,
2007:307–8, 316

blacks *(continued)*

health insurance and, **2005:**14

homelessness and, **2005:**286,
2007:316

housing and, **2004:**18–19, 277,
2006:211, 484, **2007:**287

hunger and, **2005:**286, **2007:**316

Hurricane Katrina and,
2005:341–44, 395–96, 406–7

image by, **2007:**281–83, 423–24,
462–63, 465

income and, **2004:**291, **2006:**280

independents and, **2004:**368,
2007:281

inflation and, **2006:**484

Iraq war and, **2004:**368–69,
2006:108, 279, **2007:**83, 316

Jackson, Michael, and,
2005:91–92, 157–58

Kerry, John, and, **2004:**333

law enforcement and,
2004:288–90, **2005:**420

liberals and, **2004:**103

marriage and, **2004:**86–87,
223–24

Medicaid and, **2005:**14

Medicare and, **2000:**280, **2005:**14

Middle East and, **2006:**122–24

money and, **2006:**484

morality and, **2005:**136,
2007:239, 304, 316

mortality of, **2004:**291

most important issues for,
2006:279, 281, **2007:**316

most important national leader in
black community today [list],
2003:251–52, 297

national security and, **2007:**316

oil and, **2005:**286, **2006:**484

opportunities and, **2001:**147, 152,
2004:18–19, 276–78, 317–18,
377, **2005:**287, 314

party identification and, **2006:**276,
2007:281

Persian Gulf War and, **2004:**369

pets and, **2007:**518

political affiliation and,
2005:183–84, 264–65, 342,
2006:253, 276, 297–98, 355,
378, **2007:**281

position of, **2004:**66–67, 130,
2005:20, 22, 39

poverty and, **2004:**291–92,
2005:286, 394, **2007:**316

predictions for, **1998:**222

Protestantism and, **2007:**83

race relations and, **2000:**281,
2004:66–67, 274–76, 292–94,
350–51

racial profiling and, **2004:**288–90

religion and, **2004:**120, 512,
2005:133, 233, 447, **2006:**108,
355, 494

Republican Party and, **2000:**280,
282, **2004:**318, 368, **2007:**281

retirement and, **2006:**484

safety and, **2004:**18–19

satisfaction of, **2001:**29, 146–47,
158, **2003:**360, **2004:**18–19,
66–67, **2005:**20, 22, 39,
2007:289–90, 292–94, 554

school and, **2004:**455–56,
2005:351

Simpson, O. J., and, **2005:**92,
157–58

Social Security and, **2000:**281

sports and, **2004:**44

Supreme Court and, **2005:**345

taxes and, **2000:**280, **2007:**304

terrorism and, **2006:**279,
2007:316

think few black people dislike
whites, **2003:**220

unemployment and, **2005:**286

U.S., satisfaction with, **2004:**
316–17, **2006:**81–82, 238

violent groups at school and,
1999:189

vote for black presidential nominee, **1999:**53
wages and, **2006:**484
Blair, Jayson, 2003:176, **2004:**394
Blair, Tony, 2001:278, **2002:**400,
2003:454, **2004:**210, 513,
2006:70–71, 536, **2007:**88
know name (Blair) of prime minister of England, **2000:**176
opinion of, **1998:**155, **2001:**233,
2002:295
blogs, 2006:54–56
blue states
Bush, George W., and, **2004:**184,
189
economy and, **2004:**333–35
election of 2004 and, **2004:**162,
184, 189, 333–36, 338–40,
354, 430
Iraq war and, **2004:**336
Kerry, John, and, **2004:**189
Nader, Ralph, and, **2004:**189
political affiliation and, **2004:**3,
23, 25
Blumenthal, Sidney, 1999:6
bobsled
as favorite Winter Olympic event,
2002:36
body mass index (BMI), 2003:419,
2004:485–87
Bogart, Humphrey, 2001:77
Bonaparte, Napoleon, 2000:141,
155
Bonds, Barry, 1998:226, **2003:**198,
2004:144, 487, **2005:**115, **2007:**1,
261
Bono, 2005:482, **2006:**536
books
how much information about
health or medicine you get
from, **2002:**293
trust and confidence in health and
medicine information from,
2002:293

boredom, 2004:26, 466
Bork, Robert, 2005:238, 283, 328,
424
born again Christianity, 2004:119,
358–59
Bosnia
approve of presence of U.S. troops
in, **1998:**157
See also Kosovo situation
bosses, 2002:138–39
should have access to genetic
information, **2001:**162
Boston, 2000:298–99, **2001:**235,
2004:448–49
Boston Globe
heard or read about columnist
Patricia Smith making up
quotes in, **1998:**194
Boston Red Sox, 2001:81
Boston University, 2003:299
bounce (in polls)
after conventions, **2004:**278–80,
311–14, 320–24, 327–28,
356–58, 378–79, 396–97, 444
after elections, **2004:**450–52,
504
Bourque, Ray, 2001:142
Bowl Championship Series,
2004:487–89
bowling, 2004:44
as favorite sport to watch,
1998:237, **2000:**136
hobby you are particularly interested in, **2002:**6
boxing, 2004:44, 489, **2007:**24
as favorite sport to watch,
1998:237, **2000:**136
Boyd, Kenneth Lee, 2005:456
Boy Scouts of America
allow openly gay adults to serve
as leaders, **2000:**199
Bradley, Bill, 2004:5, 41
chances of, **1999:**101, **2000:**27,
36, 49

Bradley, Bill *(continued)*
  characteristics of, **1999:**102, 113,
    2000:27, 37, 49, 57
  Gallup analysis of his candidacy,
    1999:86
  likely to support, **1998:**66, 227–28,
    1999:72, 84, 101, 118–20,
    2000:9–10, 26, 29, 33, 49,
    53–54, 68, **2001:**192, **2002:**90
  opinion of, **1998:**65, **1999:**46,
    101, **2000:**44
  qualifications of, **1999:**101–2,
    2000:27, 36, 49, 57
  and town meeting, **1999:**101
Bradley, Omar, **2000:**410
Brady Bill, **2004:**472
Brady Campaign, **2004:**472
Brahimi, Lakhdar, **2004:**174, 178
Braun, Carol Moseley, **2003:**252,
    2004:5, 11
  likely to support, **2003:**135, 190,
    215–16, 277, 323, 335,
    374–75, 382, 390, 417,
    432–33, 446–47
  opinion of, **2003:**306
  as second choice for nomination,
    2003:335
Brazil, **1998:**79, 180, **2000:**173,
    2001:35, 43, 84, **2004:**73
Bremer, Paul, **2004:**210, 263
The Bridge on the River Kwai
    (movie), **1998:**187
Brigham Young University (BYU),
    2003:299
British Medical Journal, **2004:**191
Brokaw, Tom, **2007:**193
Brooks, Garth, **2000:**265
Brown, Jerry, **2004:**42, **2007:**355
Brown, Michael, **2005:**336–37, 343
Brown, Ron, **2003:**252
Brown, Sherrod, **2006:**364
Brown, Tina, **1998:**194
Brownback, Sam, **2005:**142, 300,
    310, **2007:**113–14, 326

chances of winning nomination,
    2007:239
  evolution and, **2007:**250
  geographic region and, **2007:**344
  guns and, **2007:**222
  image of, **2007:**362
Browne, Harry, **2000:**161, 182, 397
Brown University, **2003:**299
Brown v. Board of Education,
    2004:199–201
Bryant, Kobe, **2000:**289, **2001:**142,
    2003:280–81, **2004:**53–54, 367,
    394
Buchanan, Pat
  likely to support, **1998:**65,
    1999:71, 84, 88–89, 99,
    2000:78, 115, 139, 161, 181,
    197–98, 223, 236
  opinion of, **1998:**64, **1999:**46,
    2000:182
  used Internet to visit his Web site,
    2000:397
budget, federal
  approval ratings, **1998:**228, **2002:**
    91, **2005:**15–16, 19, 27, 68, 425
  balanced, **1998:**162, **1999:**80–81,
    2000:24, **2001:**8–9, 22,
    2002:130
  Bush, George W., and, **1999:**81,
    2000:24, 196, **2002:**33,
    2004:56, 111–12, 420,
    2005:3–4, 15–16, 19, 27,
    31–32, 39, 68, 155, 425
  Clinton and, **1998:**55–56, **1999:**92
  concern for, **2004:**58, 147, 271–72
  Congress and, **1999:**142
  defense spending in, **2002:**34, 51,
    2004:97–98
  Democratic Party and, **2001:**210,
    2007:16–17, 192
  economy and, **2004:**150,
    2006:216, 222, **2007:**10
  election of 2004 and,
    2004:111–12, 170, 420

election of 2006 and, **2006:**455,
460–61, 478
Gore and, **2000:**195
and government shutdown,
1998:204–5, **1999:**141
Hurricane Katrina and, **2005:**352,
354
independents and, **2007:**16–17, 192
investors and, **2004:**40, 261,
271–72
Kerry, John, and, **2004:**111–12,
420
on military, **1998:**236
as most important issue, **2004:**
37–38, 113, 155–56, 246,
466–67, **2005:**3–4, 38, 45, 99,
113, 148, 152, 174, 198, 213,
220, 304, 347, 365–66, 421,
2006:2–3, 68–69, 138–39, 237,
288, 338, 479, **2007:**37–38, 54,
410–12, 442–43, 532
political affiliation and,
2004:15–16, 38, 156,
2007:16–17, 192
predictions for, **1998:**3–4, 162,
252, **2001:**105–6
president and, **2007:**2, 16–17,
60–61, 90, 191–92, 237–38,
305
as priority, **1998:**235, **2000:**428,
2007:2, 16–17, 60–61, 90,
148–49, 191–92, 237–38, 305
Republican Party and,
1998:55–56, **1999:**92,
2001:210, **2007:**16–17, 192
spending increases and,
1998:236–37
State of the Union on, **1998:**162
and tax cuts, **2001:**119
as voting issue, **2003:**454
budget deficit, federal
approve of, **2002:**22, 34
Bush, George W., and, **2002:**27
causes of, **2002:**22

Clinton and, **1998:**2, 157, 162,
1999:44
credit for reduction in, **1998:**3
as crisis, **2003:**271
Democratic Party and, **2002:**18,
27, 171, **2003:**5, 272
as most important issue, **1998:**60,
1999:194–95, **2000:**191,
2001:58, 121, 255, **2002:**9, 70,
116, 224, 359, **2003:**25, 61, 86,
122, 155, 203, 284, 401, 442
as most important issue facing
nation 25 years from now,
2002:117
predictions for, **2001:**206
as priority, **2000:**212, 428,
2002:17, **2003:**4
reduction in, credit for, **1998:**2–3
Republican Party and, **1998:**2–3,
157, 162, **2002:**18, 171,
2003:5, 272
responsibility for, **2002:**21–22
as serious problem, **1998:**157
tax cuts and, **2001:**39, 60–61,
2002:22, **2003:**152–53,
271–72
use surplus federal money to pay
down debt, **1998:**4
as voting issue, **1998:**159,
2003:338–39, 416, 454
budget surplus, federal
Bush, George W., and, **2000:**242,
248, 258, 275, 309
decrease in, **2001:**206
Gore and, **2000:**242, 248, 258,
275, 309
uses for, **1998:**4, **2000:**318
as voting issue, **2000:**19, 72, 243
building contractors
honesty and ethical standards of,
1999:148, **2000:**389, **2002:**373
Bullock, Kenneth, 2004:505
Bullock, Sandra, 2000:99,
2001:76–77, **2006:**507

Bureau of Labor Statistics,
2004:340
Burns, Conrad, 2006:364, 462
Bush, Barbara, 1998:2, 154,
1999:242, 2000:29, 431,
2001:278, 2002:400, 2003:455,
2004:513–14, 2005:483
Bush, George H. W.
admiration of, 1998:1, 154,
1999:242, 2002:400,
2003:454, 2004:230, 514,
2005:482
approval ratings, 1998:25,
1999:63, 2002:96, 2004:7–8,
17, 113, 124, 151, 211–12,
229–32, 247–48, 258–59, 265,
303, 414, 416, 422, 444,
2005:26, 33–34, 48–51, 118,
417, 2006:6, 40–41, 96, 170,
182, 190, 200–201, 245–46,
329, 466, 539, 2007:26, 100,
313
after two years in office (Oct.
1990), 2002:387
averages during seventh quar-
ter as president, 2002:322
in December of last year in
office, *Gallup analysis* of,
2000:422
quarterly averages, 2002:111
volatility in, *Gallup analysis*
of, 1998:22–23
and Clinton, 1998:168
conventions and, 2004:279–80,
313, 356–57
Democratic Party and,
2004:211–12, 229–30, 238
domestic problems, time with,
2004:7
dynasty and, 2007:513
economy and, 1999:63, 2000:262,
267, 2004:85, 258, 2005:33
in elections, 2007:101, 269
energy and, 2006:170

ethics of, 2005:399
foreign affairs and, 2004:7,
2005:34
gender and, 2004:96
Gallup analysis of gender gap,
versus Clinton/Dukakis,
2000:159
as greatest president, 2000:58,
2001:44, 2003:163–64, 413,
2004:233, 2007:76
image of, 2004:233, 237–38, 249
independents and, 2004:211–12,
229–30, 238
legacy of, 2006:518
as outstanding president, 1999:77
Persian Gulf War and, 2004:124,
230
political affiliation and, 2005:52,
2006:190, 246, 537
Quayle, Dan, and, 2004:273
re-election failure of, 2004:8, 17,
85, 113, 124–26, 151, 259,
265, 387
Republican Party and,
2004:211–12, 229–30, 238
State of the Union address of,
2004:19, 29, 2005:50–52
U.S., satisfaction with, and,
2004:239, 341–42
Weinberger, Caspar, and,
2007:115
as worst president, 2000:59
Bush, George W.
abortion and, 2000:242, 248, 258,
275, 428, 2003:394–95,
2004:140–41, 169–70, 329,
383–84, 428, 471, 473–74,
2005:3–4, 156, 176
accomplishments of, 2005:27, 37
admiration of, 2000:60, 431,
2001:37, 278, 2002:137, 399,
2003:225, 407, 454,
2004:320–22, 351–52, 513–14
advertising and, 2004:346

age and, **2004:**137–38, 184–85,
205, 379, 442–43, **2005:**156,
2006:215, 316, 530
agrees with you on issues,
1999:65, 106, **2000:**70, 84,
248, 257, 276, 332, **2001:**37,
228, **2002:**136–37, **2003:**225
AIDS and, **2005:**72
airline strike and, **2001:**85
al Qaeda and, **2004:**134–35,
146–47, 167–68
approval ratings, **2001:**48, 86,
145, 228, **2002:**14–15, 27, 56,
111, 141, 153, 168, 173, 187,
211, 215, 270, 319, 357, 382,
387, **2003:**14, 83–86, 103,
106–7, 113, 139, 151–52, 172,
185, 208–9, 225, 247, 256,
265–66, 277, 301, 305, 311,
319, 332, 366, 390, 438, 446,
2004:6–8, 12, 16–18, 20,
48–50, 52–53, 58–61, 64, 68,
75–76, 95–96, 104–5, 112–13,
121, 124, 133–35, 137–39,
145, 151, 162–63, 166–68,
184–85, 187–89, 191, 193,
196–97, 205, 210–12, 217–18,
222, 229–30, 235–36, 240–42,
257–60, 265–67, 282, 284,
297–98, 302–3, 335, 342, 346,
354, 357–58, 389, 391, 397,
405–6, 413–14, 416, 418,
421–23, 430, 437, 444, 450,
452, 504, **2005:**11–12, 15–16,
18–20, 24–31, 33–34, 38–39,
41, 48–52, 59–60, 62–64,
68–69, 87–90, 98–99, 102–3,
111–14, 118–20, 130–31,
141–42, 155–57, 164–67, 169,
173, 193–94, 212, 214, 227,
236, 239, 242–43, 252,
262–64, 273, 278, 280–81,
296–97, 317–18, 320–21,
325–26, 337, 342, 345–46,

351–53, 359, 375, 384,
391–93, 397, 402, 417–18,
424–26, 428, 433–34, 445,
451, 461–62, 464, 471,
2006:5–7, 23–24, 29, 40–43,
46, 53–54, 61, 91–93, 95–98,
105, 116–17, 120–21, 139–40,
154–56, 169–72, 174, 181–83,
186–90, 193, 196–97,
200–221, 240–41, 243–44,
262–63, 276, 302–4, 309,
315–16, 328–29, 347–48,
352–53, 374–75, 382–83, 387,
398, 404, 421–22, 433–34,
443, 465–66, 468, 476,
515–16, 518, 530–31, 539,
2007:13–14, 25–26, 52–53,
65–66, 86–87, 100, 115–16,
152, 166–67, 200–202,
210–11, 224–25, 270–72,
280–81, 297–99, 312–13, 359,
365–67, 400, 408–9, 413, 415,
418, 439–40, 480–82, 484–86,
501–2, 529
abortion and, **2002:**92
after two years in office (Dec.
2002), **2002:**387
averages during seventh quar-
ter as president, **2002:**322
budget and, **2002:**91,
2003:113, 311
campaign finance and, **2002:**91
Chinese plane and, **2001:**92
and defense, **2002:**91
domestic problems and,
2003:266
economy and, **2001:**55, 68,
102, 166, 228, **2002:**27, 57,
91, 153, 332, 350, 357,
387–88, **2003:**14, 92, 113,
144, 152, 209, 247–48, 256,
266, 311, 319, 366
education and, **2001:**166,
2002:91, 215

Bush, George W. *(continued)*
energy and, **2002:**92, **2003:**92,
311
environment and, **2001:**68,
102, 166, **2002:**92, **2003:**92
explaining his policies and
plans for the future,
2001:169
factors affecting, **2001:**169,
2002:157–58, 211
faith-based organizations and,
2001:166
finance reform and, **2001:**167
foreign affairs and, **2001:**56,
166, 228, **2002:**27, 43, 57,
91, 153, 215, 351, 357, 388,
2003:113, 132, 152, 209,
248, 256–57, 266, 311,
319– **2003:**320, 366
healthcare and, **2002:**92, 215,
2003:305, 311
image of America and,
2001:139, 180
Iraq and, **2002:**285, 308, 388,
2003:113, 209, 248, 257,
266, 311, 320, 366
Medicare and, **2003:**305, 311
Middle East and, **2002:**92,
133, **2003:**200, 209
nuclear weapons policy and,
2002:92
patients' bill of rights and,
2001:166
as a person, **2003:**407
personal, **2001:**7, 36, 168
prescription drugs and,
2001:166
presidential transition and,
2001:7, 19
quarterly approval, **2002:**321
quarterly averages for,
2002:111
relationship of ratings on
issues to, **2003:**311

Social Security and, **2001:**166,
2002:91
taxes and, **2001:**110, 166, 179,
2002:92, **2003:**113, 311
terrorism and, **2001:**226, 250,
254, 269, **2002:**91–92, 153,
2003:305, 310, 320
unemployment and, **2002:**92
automobile ownership and,
2004:440–41
and bipartisanship, **2000:**70,
2002:137, 216
blacks and, **2002:**393,
2004:184–85
blue states and, **2004:**184, 189
budget and, **1999:**81, **2000:**24,
242, 248, 258, 275, 309, 428,
2001:206, **2002:**21, **2004:**56,
111–12, 420, **2005:**3–4, 15–16,
19, 27, 31–32, 39, 68, 155, 425
business and, **2004:**104
Cabinet of, **2001:**7, 19, **2004:**479–81
and campaign finance reform,
2001:71
campaign finance reform and,
2000:86, 428
can name him as your party's
nominee, **2000:**90
capabilities of, **1999:**65, 82,
2000:26, 35, **2001:**20, 36
cares about needs of people like
you, **1999:**65, 82, 105,
2000:22, 84, 142, 248, 257,
276, 332, 358, **2001:**37, 168,
228, **2002:**136, 216, 358,
2003:225, 407
Catholicism and, **2004:**217–18,
328–29, 428–29, 442–43
chances of, **1999:**101, **2000:**26,
35, 46, 60
change and, **2000:**23
characteristics of, **2000:**23, 36, 57,
358, **2001:**20, 36, 106, 168,
228, **2002:**137–38

character ratings of, **2004:**82–84,
308–9, 320–23, 351–52,
371–73, 398–99, **2006:**42–43,
97, 187, 353
Cheney, Dick, and, **2000:**232,
2001:7, **2003:**272, 400,
2004:124, 126, 273, 353–54,
2006:95
children and, **2005:**72
church and, **2004:**332–33, 442–43
civil unions and, **2004:**442–43
and Clinton, **2005:**425
Clinton and, **2001:**12
cloning and, **2002:**145–46
community and, **2004:**442–43
compassion and, **2001:**20,
2003:53
confidence in, **2000:**228, **2001:**48,
216, **2002:**27, **2003:**46, 123,
152, **2004:**29, **2005:**425,
2006:39, 62, 514–15,
2007:204–5, 306–7, 393, 418
confidence in, trust more what he
says than you trusted other
presidents in office,
2003:225–26
as conservative, **2000:**248, 277,
2001:106, **2003:**53, **2004:**
102–3, 133, 318–20
conservatives and, **2004:**184,
441–42
conventions and, **2004:**278–80,
297, 312–13, 320–24, 351–52,
354, 356–58, 371–73, 378,
444, 498–99
corporations and, **2002:**190, 192,
197, 216, **2003:**140, **2005:**156
corporatoins and, **2002:**189
cost of living and, **2005:**155
crime and, **1999:**81, **2000:**24, 86,
143, 428
death penalty and, **2000:**202
debates and, **2000:**61, 326, 332,
336, 345, **2004:**395–96, 398,

400–403, 406, 409–11, 416,
444, 498–99
decision making and, **2001:**20, 106
defeat of, desire for, **2004:**32–33,
41, 383–84, 422, 430–31,
497–99
defense and, **2000:**248, 258, 275,
293, 428, **2004:**97, 269–70,
352, 355, 358, 383–84, 395
democracy and, **2005:**72–73
Democratic Party and,
2000:427–28, **2004:**68, 77, 84,
92, 104, 112, 134–35, 145–46,
184–85, 211–12, 229–30, 238,
282, 319–20, 337–38, 360,
375, 395, 401–2, 409, 422,
442, 450, 479, 504, 514
DNA evidence and, **2005:**72
doing bad job, get him out of
office, as most important issue
in deciding your vote for president in 2004, **2003:**416
domestic problems, time with,
2004:7
drugs and, **1999:**106
DUI arrest and, **2000:**365–66
dynasty and, **2007:**513
and economy, **2002:**22
economy and, **1999:**80, 96, 116,
2000:26, 35, 47, 206, 309, 357,
428, **2001:**275, **2002:**216, 223,
2003:14, 17–18, 53, 78, 140,
248, **2004:**6–7, 12, 14–15, 20,
29, 49, 58, 64–65, 85, 107,
111–12, 139, 171–72, 187–88,
191, 196, 236, 255, 257–59,
301–2, 321–22, 334, 347,
351–52, 355, 358, 374–75,
381–84, 389, 394, 397–99,
402, 409–10, 418–21, 432,
444, 450, 452, 469, 497–99,
2005:27, 29, 37
education and, **1999:**81, 116,
2000:24, 85, 143, 242, 248,

Bush, George W. *(continued)*
  258, 275, 309, 357, 428,
  2004:7, 112, 184–85, 301–2,
  317–18, 348, 352, 376,
  383–84, 409–10, 420, 427,
  442–43, 469, 498–99,
  2005:3–4, 15–16, 19, 27, 29,
  31–32, 37, 39, 48, 65–67,
  156–57
  elderly and, **2000:**428,
    2004:383–84
  election of 2000 and, **2000:**78,
    182, 250, **2001:**20, **2004:**41, 87,
    96, 315–16, 337–38, 442–43,
    2007:21, 113, 253, 269
    Gallup analysis of closeness of
      popular vote, **2000:**367
  election of 2004 and, **2003:**136,
    2004:6–8, 11–12, 15–16, 32,
    41, 48–50, 60–61, 69, 75–77,
    82–85, 111–12, 124–26,
    132–34, 140–41, 156–57,
    161–63, 171–72, 184–85,
    188–89, 196–97, 229–30,
    256–60, 267–70, 283–85,
    297–302, 308–9, 311–12,
    318–24, 326, 332–35, 337–40,
    345–47, 351–52, 354–58,
    371–75, 378–79, 381–84,
    388–90, 395–4402
  election of 2006 and, **2005:**397,
    429
  Elían González situation handled
    by, **2000:**131
  employment and, **2000:**242, 248,
    2004:14–15, 58, 111–12,
    382–84, 469
  energy and, **2001:**68, 102, 156,
    2002:351, **2004:**121, 139, 235,
    2007:52–53, 122
  Enron and, **2002:**31–32
  environment and, **1999:**81,
    2000:24, 85, 242, 248, 428,
    2001:102, 181, **2004:**138–40,

    469, **2005:**3–4, 15–16, 19, 27,
    29, 37, 39, 156
  ethics and, **2005:**276–77, 398–99,
    402
  expectations of, **2000:**196
  familiarity with, **2004:**83–84
  family's campaigning on his behalf
    in New Hampshire, **2000:**29
  feelings about, **2004:**104, 117
  finances and, **2007:**486
  first term of, **2005:**27–29, 37
  foreign affairs and, **1999:**81, 106,
    116, **2000:**24, 85, 143, 242,
    248, 275, 428, **2004:**6–7, 49,
    85, 91–92, 101–2, 111–12,
    188, 383–84, 389, 450
  foreign aid and, **2005:**156
  foreign image of, **2004:**91–92
  foreign trade and, **2000:**248,
    2005:155
  gasoline and, **2000:**86, 309, 320,
    2004:222, **2005:**130, 155,
    168–69, 325, 346, 422
  gender and, **2000:**197,
    2004:95–97, 184–85, 332–33,
    384, 395, 402, 442–43,
    2006:215, 316, 348, 530,
    2007:253
    Gallup analysis of gender gap,
      versus Gore, **2000:**159, 166
  geographic region and, **2006:**215,
    316, 530
  government and, **1999:**82,
    2000:22, 84, 142, 248, 257,
    276, 332, 357, **2001:**228,
    2002:137, 216, **2005:**156,
    374–75, 425
  as greatest president,
    2003:163–64, 413, **2004:**233,
    2007:76
  guns and, **1999:**81, **2000:**24, 85,
    143, 242, 248, 258, 275
  Harken Energy Corporation and,
    2002:197

has clear plan for solving country's problems, **2002:**358, **2003:**225

healthcare and, **1999:**81, **2000:**24, 85, 143, 242, 248, 258, 275, 309, 428, **2004:**7, 21, 29, 49–50, 104, 109–12, 301–2, 321–22, 374–75, 381–84, 389, 398–99, 409–10, 419–21, 432, 445, 450, 469, 498–99, **2005:**3–4, 15–16, 19, 27, 29, 31–32, 37, 39, 52, 65–67, 130, 156–57, 325

health insurance and, **2004:**471

Hispanics and, **2004:**329

homeland security and, **2004:**104

homelessness and, **2000:**25, 428

homosexuality and, **2004:**85, 104–6, 111–12, 329, 369, 469, 471, **2005:**188

honesty of, **1999:**82, **2000:**85, 248, 257, 276, 332, 354, 358, **2001:**36, 168, **2002:**137, 216, **2003:**225, 407, **2004:**82–84, 104, 138, 145, 172, 308–9, 320–23, 351–52, 371–73, 383–84, 399, 497–99, **2005:**32–33, 276–77, 280, 300, 352, 402, 425

Hurricane Katrina and, **2005:**331, 337, 341–47, 351–53, 393, **2007:**473

Hussein, Saddam, and, **2004:**135

ideology and, **2004:**133, 318–20, 441–42, **2005:**309–10, 417

image of, **2004:**49, 91–92, 112, 133, 162–63, 210, 233, 237–38, 249, 259–60, 272, 284–85, 288, 298, 318–24, 351–52, 354, 358, 371–73, 402, 406, 411–12, 445, 479–80, **2006:**75–76, 186–87, 190–91, 330, 422

image of America and, **2001:**139, 180, **2005:**27, 29, 37, 39

immigration and, **2004:**14–15, 21, 420, **2005:**3–4, 15–16, 19, 72, 156–57, 425, 451

inauguration of, **2001:**18

income and, **2004:**184–85, **2006:**215

independents and, **2004:**68, 112, 134–35, 145–46, 184–85, 211–12, 229–30, 238, 337–38, 352, 360, 375, 395, 402, 409, 422, 442, 450, 479, 504

inflation and, **2005:**155

influence of, **2000:**355, **2001:**37

as inspiring, **1999:**65, 82, 106, **2000:**23, 85, **2001:**37, 228, **2002:**216

intelligence system and, **2006:**144

intelligent design and, **2005:**354

interested in hearing live speech by, **2001:**79–80

investors and, **2004:**347

Iran and, **2006:**62

Iraq and, **2002:**279, 366, **2003:**45–46, 48, 53–54, 248, **2004:**29, 135, 144, **2005:**149–50

victory speech, heard or watched how much of it, **2003:**141

Iraq war and, **2003:**383, **2004:**17, 20, 49, 52–53, 104, 111–12, 115–17, 124, 146–47, 155, 171–72, 188, 194, 196–99, 211, 219, 240–42, 257–58, 260, 267–68, 301–2, 308, 321–22, 335–37, 351, 355, 358, 374–75, 381–84, 389, 395, 397–402, 418–21, 432, 437–38, 444, 450, 469, 497–99

Israel and, **2004:**389, **2007:**110, 508

Judaism and, **2004:**217–18

judicial system and, **2005:**72, 130, 156

Bush, George W. *(continued)*
know, **2000**:90
know name (Bush) of governor of
Texas, **2000**:34
leadership and, **2000**:21, 23, 47,
70, 84, 115, 142, 237, 247–48,
256–57, 276, 303, 332, 353,
358, **2001**:7, 36, 139, 168, 228,
2002:136, 216, **2003**:225, 407,
2004:82–84, 112, 308–9,
320–23, 351–52, 355, 358,
371–73, 381–82, 389, 397,
399, 444, 498–99, **2005**:425
leaders of other countries have
respect for him, **2002**:42,
2003:65, 132
as liberal, **2004**:133
liberals and, **2004**:184–85, 441–42
likely to support, **1998**:65, 227,
2000:7–10, 17, 26, 28, 44, 50,
53–54, 59, 62, 68–69, 75,
77–78, 82–83, 105, 114–15,
138–39, 161, 181, 197–98,
202, 223, 231–32, 235–36,
2001:193, **2003**:336, 447–48
presidential election, **1998**:228
marriage and, **2004**:85, 104–6,
111–12, 329, 369, 442–43, 469,
471, **2005**:3–4, 65–67, 72, 188
and McCain, **2000**:47, 50, 60, 70
media and, **2004**:433–34
Medicare and, **2000**:25, 85, 143,
242, 248, 258, 275, 309, 357,
428, **2003**:229–30,
2004:38–39, 109–10, 137–38,
352, 420, 469, **2005**:27, 29, 37,
39, 156, **2007**:38
Middle East and, **2000**:343,
2002:94, 133, 182, **2003**:182,
2007:508
military and, **2000**:428, **2001**:221,
2002:68, **2005**:32, 37, 39, 209
minorities and, **2000**:428
moderates and, **2004**:184–85, 442

morality and, **1999**:65, 105,
2000:22, 36, 85, **2002**:137,
2004:82–84, 383–84, 447–48,
469–72, 497–99, **2005**:27, 29,
37, 39, 130, 156
as most important issue, **2005**:45,
113, 152, 198, 366, 421
and most important issues,
2004:246–47, 414
music and, **2004**:440–41
national defense and, **2007**:96
National Guard service and,
2004:76–77, 387, 392–94
national security and, **2002**:168,
2004:382–84, 497–99,
2005:27, 29, 39
natural disasters and, **2005**:15,
2007:473
nonwhites and, **2004**:442–43
oil and, **2005**:155
opinion of, **1998**:64, **2000**:23, 44,
143, 146, 182, 247, 274, 311,
332, 353, 378, 404,
2001:19–20, 139, **2002**:154,
216, 295, **2003**:186, 273
opportunities and, **2000**:86
Palestinian Authority and,
2007:110, 508
partisanship and, **2005**:27, 29,
37, 39
party identification and, **2006**:29
patients' bill of rights and,
2001:141, 144
personal qualities of, **2004**:82–84,
112, 308–9, 320–23, 351–52,
358, 371–73, 383–84, 398–99,
402–3, 409, 497–99
plans of, **2005**:31–33, 41, 131,
236, 240, 242, 464, 471
policies of, **2002**:28, 353,
2003:53, **2006**:42–43, 45, 54,
92–93, 116–17, 139–40,
154–56, 186–88, 200–204,
243–44, 277, 303, 348, 422

political affiliation and,
    2006:41–42, 45–47, 54, 96,
    105, 121, 155–56, 172, 183,
    189–90, 197, 214–15, 241,
    244, 262–63, 303, 316, 318,
    330, 348, 374–75, 390–91,
    401–2, 421, 448–50, 515–16,
    530, 537
poverty and, **1999:**105, **2000:**25,
    2004:111–12, **2005:**3–4, 156
predictions for, **2002:**388
prescription drugs and, **2000:**309
presidency and, **2005:**27, 29, 37,
    39
priorities of, **2000:**428, **2001:**141,
    229, **2004:**40
privacy and, **2000:**86, **2004:**112
problems of raising children and,
    2000:25, 85, 309
Protestantism and, **2004:**217–18,
    442–43
puts country's interests ahead of
    his own, **2000:**143, 277,
    2002:137
qualifications of, **1999:**106, 116,
    2000:23, 47, 60, 85, 237, 247,
    354, **2001:**135
race and, **2004:**184–85, 442–43,
    2005:3–4, 263–64, 341–44,
    346, **2006:**215, 276, 297, 410,
    458–60, 530
race relations and, **2000:**258
red states and, **2004:**189
re-election of
    desire for, **2004:**383–84, 422,
        430–31, 497–99
    merit for, **2002:**290,
        2003:373–74, **2004:**411
    potential for, **2004:**6, 11–12,
        17, 124–26, 184–85, 193,
        210–12, 229–30, 239, 259,
        265–66, 297–98, 303,
        341–42, 357–58, 387,
        413–14, 416, 430

religion and, **1999:**106,
    2004:217–18, 255–57, 328–29,
    383–84, 428–29, 442–43,
    497–99, 505
Republican Party and, **2000:**70,
    2004:68, 104, 112, 134–35,
    145–46, 184, 211–12, 229–30,
    238, 282, 319–20, 324,
    337–38, 360, 375, 395, 401–2,
    409, 422, 442, 450, 479, 504,
    514
residential area and, **2006:**215
respect for, **2000:**23, **2001:**169
Rumsfeld, Donald, and, **2004:**504
satisfaction with, **2000:**9, 15
scandals and, **2005:**32
Schiavo, Terri, and, **2005:**105,
    109–10, 112, 122, 131
school and, **2004:**471
science and, **2004:**139–40
September 11, 2001, terrorist
    attacks and, **2004:**104, 144–47,
    211, 230, 267, 325–26,
    2005:26–27
shares your values, **2000:**22, 84,
    142, 248, 256, 276, 281, 332,
    358, **2002:**136, 216, 357–58,
    2003:407
Social Security and, **2000:**25, 85,
    143, 183, 242, 248, 258, 275,
    309, 357, 428, **2004:**21, 29,
    110–12, 420, 469, 471,
    2007:38
as someone you would be proud
    to have as president, **2000:**70,
    84, 248, 257, 276
space program and, **2004:**20–21,
    82
special interest groups and,
    2004:82–83
State of the Union Speech and,
    2001:48, **2002:**29, **2004:**
    19–21, 28–29, **2006:**40–42,
    45, **2007:**28, 38

Bush, George W. *(continued)*
stem cell research and, **2004:**329, 471, **2005:**72, 194–95, 306, **2006:**298
support for, **2000:**60, **2001:**7, **2002:**130, 320–21, **2003:**16, 78, 134–35, 214, 257, 310, 320, 374, 390, 415
swing states and, **2004:**189, 374–75, 430, 442
swing voters and, **2004:**282–83, 436
tax cuts and, **2000:**288, 428, **2001:**23, 39, 49, 124, 195, **2003:**140, 152, 175, 185
taxes and, **2000:**24, 36, 85, 143, 242, 248, 258, 275, 288, 309, 357, 428, **2001:**38, **2004:**7, 29, 49, 104, 112, 153, 301–2, 321–22, 352, 355, 383–84, 409–10, 420, 469, 471, 498–99, **2005:**3–4, 6–7, 15–16, 19, 27, 29, 37–39, 65–67, 155
teenagers and, **2004:**391, 414
terrorism and, **2001:**220–21, 273, **2002:**216, **2003:**14, 53, 248, **2004:**20, 29, 104, 111, 124, 134–35, 144–47, 167–68, 171–72, 188, 197, 219, 258–59, 267–68, 301–2, 321–22, 325–26, 351–52, 358, 374–75, 381–84, 389, 397–99, 402, 418–21, 432, 437–38, 444, 450, 469, 497–99
Texas and, **2000:**247
top priority of his programs (by ideology) [list], **2001:**9
torture and, **2005:**441, **2006:**393
in touch with average voter, **2000:**36, 357, **2001:**169, **2003:**140
understanding of, **2004:**171–72
understands complex issues, **2000:**23, 143, 248, 257, 277,

332, 357, **2001:**37, 228, **2002:**137, 216, 358
unemployment and, **2005:**3–4, 155
United Nations and, **2004:**101–2
U.S., satisfaction with, and, **2004:**239, 341–42
used Internet to visit his Web site, **2000:**397
USS *Cole* situation and, **2000:**343
vacation and, **2001:**185, **2002:**225
values and, **2004:**82–84, 308–9, 320–22, 351–52, 371–73, 383–84, 399, 469–72, 497–99, **2005:**277, 300, 425
veterans and, **2004:**84, 418–19, 442–43
vice presidential choice of, **2000:**226
Vietnam War and, **2004:**76–77, 83–84
vision and, **1999:**105, **2000:**22, 35, 60, 84, 143, 248, 257, 276, 332
voted for, **2000:**397
voting issues and, **2003:**416
weapons of mass destruction and, **2004:**53, 104, 308, **2005:**149–50, 279–80, 418
welfare and, **2005:**156
whites and, **2004:**184, 333, 442–43
Bush, Jeb, 2004:457, **2005:**310
Bush, Laura, 2001:278, **2002:**400, **2003:**455, **2004:**354, 513–14, **2005:**483
Bush daughters, 2001:140
Bush (G.W.) administration
approval ratings, **2001:**187, 250, **2002:**28, 67
big business and, **2001:**106, 169
budget and, **2001:**38
civil liberties and, **2002:**275–76, **2003:**315

confidence in, **2002:**384, **2003:**32,
45, 54
economy and, **2001:**38, **2002:**388,
2003:310
education and, **2001:**38
energy and, **2001:**38, 130
Enron and, **2002:**13, 31, 38–39,
197–98
environment and, **2001:**102
ethics and, **2002:**216
Iraq and, **2002:**258, 285, 308,
384–85, **2003:**32, 45–46, 54,
59, 95–96, 142, 183–84, 301,
321, 449
Middle East and, **2002:**133
national security and, **2001:**38
priorities of, **2003:**142, 152, 172
Social Security and, **2001:**24
tax cuts and, **2001:**38, 49, 119
terrorism and, **2003:**172–73
will be able to do the following
[list], **2001:**105–6
will it enact certain policies [list],
2001:22
business and industry,
2004:361–62, 407, **2006:**341–43,
2007:7–8, 179–80, 269–71,
385–87, 528–29
accounting and, **2004:**271–72
Bush, George W., and, **2002:**189,
2004:104
Clinton and, **2002:**189
concern for, **2004:**147, 271–72
conditions in your community,
1998:48, **2000:**190,
2003:143–44
confidence in, **1998:**182,
2000:210, **2001:**149,
2002:185, **2003:**205–6,
2004:225, 306, **2005:**201
economy and, **2002:**223,
2006:216, 222
environment and, **2000:**120
gasoline and, **2004:**222, **2006:**170

gender and, **2003:**205, **2005:**415
honesty of, **2004:**485, **2005:**448
image of, **2005:**310–13, 422
influence of, **2000:**216, **2001:**169,
2002:189
investors and, **2004:**40, 260–61,
271–72
mergers and, **2000:**42, 360
as most important issue, **2005:**
366, 421, **2006:**138–39,
479
political affiliation and, **2006:**
139, 419
recommend as career for young
man, **1998:**238
recommend as career for young
woman, **1998:**238, **2001:**109
regulation of, **2002:**192, **2003:**93,
2005:415–16, 421
small business
confidence in, **1998:**182
as threat, **1998:**240, **2000:**360,
2002:195
See also corporations
business executive(s)
greed and corruption among, and
economy, **2002:**223
honesty and ethical standards of,
2000:389, **2001:**265, **2002:**50,
373, **2003:**422–23
as presidential preparation,
2003:375
business executives, 2006:519
Bustamante, Cruz, 2003:278–79,
282–83, 343–44
Butler, Jim, 2004:330

C

Cabinet (executive), 2004:479–81
nominations to
justified for senator to oppose
nomination only because of

Cabinet (executive) *(continued)*
   policy disagreements,
      2001:17
   rate Bush's choices for,
      2001:7, 19
   too liberal or conservative,
      2001:7
   See also specific nominees
cable television, 2004:501–3
   See also television
Cage, Nicholas, 2000:99, **2001:**76
Calderon, Felipe, 2007:112
California, 2002:160, **2004:**3,
   24–25, 252–53, 307, **2005:**414
   electoral recall
      candidates in, **2003:**278–79, 343
      Clinton and, **2003:**343–44, 350
      debates in, **2003:**344
      interest in, **2003:**343, 349
      issues versus leadership in,
         2003:344
      likely voters, **2003:**278, 282,
         342–43, 349
      opinion of, **2003:**267–68, 343,
         350
      Republican Party and,
         2003:344, 350
      would vote to recall governor
         of your state, **2003:**268, 367
Calloway, Lisa, 2004:215
Camejo, Peter, 2003:278–79,
   343–44, **2004:**284, 299–300
Caminiti, Ken, 2004:488
campaign finance, 1998:167,
   2005:11, 20, 22, 40, **2006:**189
campaign finance reform
   approval ratings, **2000:**86, 344,
      2001:71, **2002:**40
   attentiveness to, **2001:**71
   Bush, George W., and, **2000:**86,
      2001:167, **2002:**91
   effects of, **2000:**344
   opinion of, **2000:**344, **2001:**71
   predictions for, **2002:**40

as priority, **2000:**428, **2001:**9, 141
   satisfaction with, **2001:**30
   as voting issue, **2000:**19, 72, 193
campaigning, negative. *See* negative
   campaigning
Canada, 2005:60–61, 79, 128,
   2006:12–13, 71, 78, 130
   crime in, **2004:**80–81
   drug use in, **2004:**55–56
   eating in, **2004:**26
   families in, **2004:**26
   healthcare in, **2004:**26–27
   homosexuality and, **2004:**404–5
   know name (Chrétien) of prime
      minister of, **2000:**176
   marriage in, **2004:**404–5
   opinion of, **2000:**173, **2001:**35, 43,
      84, **2002:**52, **2003:**56, **2004:**73
   religion in, **2004:**405, 415
   smoking in, **2004:**79–80
   stem cell research and,
      2004:415–16
   traditional values and, **2004:**57
cancer, 2004:458, **2006:**481–82, 521
   as most important issue,
      2001:121, **2003:**203, 443
   as most important issue facing
      nation 25 years from now,
      2002:117
   predictions for, **1998:**179, 222
   worry about, **2003:**424
candidates for office
   dissatisfaction with, as most
      important issue, **2001:**121,
      2002:10, 71, 116, 233, 360,
      2003:25, 62, 86, 122, 155, 203,
      284, 401, 443
canning
   hobby you are particularly inter-
      ested in, **2002:**7
Canseco, Jose, 2005:115
Cantril, Hadley, 2004:71
capital punishment. *See* death
   penalty

carbohydrates, 2004:294–95
carbon dioxide emissions, 2003:93
Cardin, Ben, 2006:416
card playing
favorite way of spending evening,
2002:6
career(s), 2004:100, 183,
2005:153–55
choice [list] recommended for
young man, 1998:238
choice [list] recommended for
young woman, 1998:238–39,
2001:109
See also employment
Carmona, Richard H., 2006:103,
301
Carnahan, Jean, 2002:340
carpentry
hobby you are particularly interested in, 2002:7
Carrey, Jim, 2001:76–77
cars. See automobile(s)
Carson, Johnny, 2000:98, 2002:146
Carter, Jimmy
admiration of, 1998:1, 2000:431,
2001:278, 2002:399–400,
2003:454, 2004:230, 513–14,
2005:482
approval ratings, 1998:24,
2002:96–97, 2004:8, 17, 151,
211–12, 229, 231–32, 247–48,
259, 265, 303, 414, 416, 444,
2005:26, 50–51, 118, 417,
2006:40–41, 53, 169–70, 182,
190, 245–46, 329, 466, 539,
2007:25, 100, 313, 484
averages during seventh quar-
ter as president, 2002:322
in December of last year in
office, Gallup analysis of,
2000:422
conventions and, 2004:279–80,
356–57
defense and, 2004:97

Democratic Party and,
2004:211–12, 229, 238, 514
economy and, 2004:85
election of, 2006:540
gender and, 2004:96
Gallup analysis of gender gap,
versus Ford/Reagan,
2000:159
as greatest president, 2000:58,
2001:44, 2003:163–64, 413,
2004:233, 2007:76
image of, 2004:233, 237–38, 249
independents and, 2004:211–12,
229, 238
interested in hearing live speech
by, 2001:79–80
legacy of, 2006:518
political affiliation and, 2005:483,
2006:190, 246, 537
primaries and, 2004:42
re-election failure of, 2004:17, 85,
151, 259, 265, 387
Republican Party and,
2004:211–12, 229, 238
U.S., satisfaction with, and,
2004:341
volatility in, Gallup analysis of,
1998:22–23
as worst president, 2000:59
Carter, Rosalynn
admiration of, 2002:400,
2003:455
Casablanca (movie), 1998:187
Casey, Bob, Jr., 2006:364
casinos, 2004:122–23
See also gambling
Castro, Fidel, 2000:176, 2002:317
casualties, 2005:327–28, 354, 388
catalogs
how often do you shop by catalog,
2001:189
Catholic Church
abortion and, 2005:125, 131–32,
150, 2006:133

Catholic Church (*continued*)
age and, **2005:**133, **2006:**196
approval ratings and,
2004:217–18
Bible in, **2006:**210, **2007:**230
birth control and, **2005:**125
Bush, George W., and,
2004:217–18, 328–29, 428–29,
442–43
child abuse and, **2005:**187
church and, **2004:**119, 225, 329,
370, 512, **2005:**131–32, 233
church attendance and,
2006:149–50, 234, **2007:**150
confidence in, **2004:**225,
2007:270
creationism and, **2004:**463
crime and, **2007:**217
death penalty and, **2004:**454–55,
2005:131–32, 150, 186
education and, **2005:**132
elections and, **2004:**255–57,
328–29, 428–29, 442–43,
2006:253
euthanasia and, **2005:**179
evolution and, **2004:**463
feelings about, **2002:**125
friendship and, **2004:**99
gender and, **2005:**132
geographic region and, **2004:**
251–53, 511, **2005:**132–33
Graham, Billy, and, **2005:**231
Hispanics and, **2004:**329
homosexuality and, **2004:**369–70
identification with, **2004:**118,
255–57, 358–59, 511
ideology and, **2005:**124–25, 133,
151
importance of, **2004:**118
importance in your life, **2002:**
390
income and, **2005:**133
Iraq war and, **2006:**108–10, 310
Kerry, John, and, **2004:**328–29,
428–29, 442–43

marriage and, **2004:**369–70
Middle East and, **2006:**124
Mormonism and, **2007:**94
party identification and, **2003:**84
political affiliation and,
2004:217–18, **2006:**253
preference for, **2000:**96, **2005:**114
Protestantism and, **2005:**150–51,
2006:196
race and, **2005:**133, 268
religion and, **2005:**233, **2006:**234
scandals in, **2004:**13–14, 251
stem cell research and, **2005:**125,
131–32, 150
suicide and, **2005:**131–32, 150,
179
Supreme Court and, **2005:**283
swing voters and, **2004:**328–29
teenagers and, **2004:**369–70
U.S., satisfaction with, **2006:**81,
238
See also Priests
cats
ownership of, **2001:**55
Catterall, Albert, 2004:405
Cavett, Dick, 2002:146
CBS, 2004:61–62, 387–88, 392–94
celebrity political activism, 2003:80
cell phones
change and
how soon would you plan to
switch providers after,
2003:430
plan to replace home or business phone with cellular
phone, **2003:**430
disturbed by, **2000:**134
hands-free devices, **2003:**431
hands-free devices and, **2003:**431
health risks of, **2000:**134
most important factor when
choosing cellular phone carrier
[list], **2003:**430
ownership of, **2000:**133,
2001:163, **2003:**429–30

restaurants and public establish-
ments forbidding people to
use, **2000:**134
use patterns, **2000:**133, **2001:**163,
2003:430
use while driving, **2000:**133,
2001:163
laws on, **2000:**134, **2001:**163
safety of, **2001:**163, **2003:**430
which of the following have you
done while driving [list],
2001:163
Census Bureau, U.S., 2000:76, 116,
2004:127–28, 291, 461
**Centers for Disease Control and
Prevention, 2001:**255, **2004:**148,
216, 385, 425, 490
Central America
what happens in, as important to
U.S., **2000:**186
certificates of deposit, 2004:314–15
Chafee, Lincoln, 2006:416, 462
Chalabi, Salem, 2004:209
**Challenger, Gray & Christmas,
2004:**58
Chan, Jackie, 2001:76
channeling
believe in, **2001:**137
charitable organizations, faith based
confidence in, **2001:**149
Charles, Prince of Wales, 1998:155,
2002:163
Chavis, Benjamin, 2003:252
cheating, 2004:192
Cheney, Dick, 2006:94–96, 144,
190–91, 236
advice of, **2004:**353–54
al Qaeda and, **2004:**287
approval ratings, **2001:**135, 254
Bush, George W., and, **2000:**
231–32, **2004:**124, 126, 273,
353–54
conventions and, **2004:**353, 357
Democratic Party and, **2004:**
287–88, 353–54

election of 2004 and, **2003:**272,
400, **2004:**124, 126, 272–73,
283–85, 287–88, 314, 353–54
health of, **2000:**232, 391,
2001:71–72, 154, **2004:**404
image of, **2004:**272, 284–85, 288,
353–54, 358, 406, 479–80
independents and, **2004:**287–88,
353
influence of, **2001:**7, 136,
2003:400
Iran and, **2007:**483
Iraq war and, **2004:**287
likely to support, **2000:**231–32,
235
opinion of, **2002:**295, **2003:**273,
399
qualifications of, **2000:**231,
2001:135, **2004:**273
Republican Party and,
2004:287–88, 353–54
weapons of mass destruction and,
2004:287
Chertoff, Michael, 2005:337
Chiang Kai-Shek, 2004:514,
2005:483
**Chiang Kai-shek, Madame,
2002:**400
Chicago, 2000:298–99, **2001:**235,
2004:448
Chicago Cubs, 2001:81
Chicago White Sox, 2001:81
child abuse, 2005:100, 162–64, 175,
187, 211–13
as most important issue, **2002:**10,
71, 116, 360, **2003:**25, 62, 86
as most important issue facing
nation 25 years from now,
2002:117
child care
provide tax credits to parents for,
as priority for using budget
surplus, **1998:**163
children
advertising and, **1998:**189

children *(continued)*

behavior of

as most important issue, **2001:**
58, 121, 255, **2002:**10, 71,
116, 233, 360, **2003:**25, 62,
87, 122, 155, 203, 284, 443

as most important issue facing
nation 25 years from now,
2002:117

boy or girl as easier to raise,
2000:430

Bush, George W., and, **2005:**72

care of, as biggest challenge you
face today, **2000:**192

Christmas and, **2005:**476–77

computers and, **1998:**189–90

death penalty for, **2004:**496

education and, **2004:**199–201,
276–77

extramarital, **2006:**212–13, 218,
2007:232

families and, **2004:**25, 127–28

have children under age 17 living
in your home, **2003:**232

ideal number of children to have,
2001:127

Internet and, **1998:**189–90

lack of parental supervision as
worst problem facing your
community, **2000:**191

lifestyle and, **2007:**379

marriage and, **2004:**132

media and, **1998:**189

morality and, **2005:**92

as most important issue,
2004:37–38, **2005:**99, 174,
213, **2006:**138–39, 237, 288,
338, 479

movies and, **1998:**187

needs of, as most important issue
facing nation 25 years from
now, **2002:**117

not raised right, as most important
issue facing nation 25 years

from now, **2002:**117

opportunities and, **2000:**204

opportunities for, **2004:**199–201,
276–77

parents and, **2004:**25–26

partisan views of, **2004:**38

popular culture and, **1998:**189

popular music and, **1998:**190

prefer to have boy or girl if only
one child, **2000:**430

problems of raising

Bush, George W., and,
2000:25, 85, 309

as presidential election issue,
2000:18, 72

race and, **2004:**276–77

raising

and gun violence, **2000:**157

as most important issue,
2002:360, **2003:**25, 62, 87,
122, 155, 203, 284, 443

support for, **1998:**190

raising them to be good people

ease of, **1998:**189

now versus 20 years ago,
1998:189

by year 2025, **1998:**219

smoking and, **2004:**80

spending on, **1998:**178

State of the Union address and,
2005:72

television and, **1998:**189,
2006:495

vacation and, **2005:**474

weight and, **2004:**385

China, 2004:73, 100, 394, **2005:**71,
78–79, 128, **2006:**76–77, 79, 90,
130

Clinton and, **1998:**75–76, 81–83,
86, 185

conflict with, as most important
issue, **2001:**121

crew members/hostages and,
2001:92

Democratic Party and, **1998:**75
human rights and, **1998:**81–83,
2000:154
Iraq and, **2003:**39
Most Favored Nation status and,
1998:87
nuclear weapons and, **1998:**78,
180, **2000:**92
opinion of, **1998:**80–81, 83, 188,
2000:91–92, 173, 380,
2001:44, 84, **2002:**43, 45, 52,
2003:56, 340
plane collision incident, **2001:**92
predictions for, **1998:**221
Taiwan and, **1998:**185
as threat, most critical, **2007:**508,
542
trade status of, **1998:**83,
2000:124, 154
World Trade Organization and,
2000:92, 124, 153–54, 162
Chiquita Banana Company
heard or read about *Cincinnati
Inquirer*'s illegally obtaining
information on, **1998:**193–94
Chirac, Jacques, 2004:73
Chiron Corporation, 2004:425
chiropractors, 2006:519
honesty and ethical standards of,
2003:422
Chocolat, **2001:**73
Chrétien, Jean, 2000:176, **2006:**71
Christian Coalition of America,
2005:142
Christianity, 2007:94, 230, 255,
480–82
Christmas and, **2005:**465–66, 478
church and, **2005:**233
euthanasia and, **2005:**179–80
paranormal and, **2005:**221
preferences for, **2005:**114
race and, **2005:**268
religion and, **2005:**233
suicide and, **2005:**179–80

values/beliefs of, as voting issue,
2003:416
Christmas, 2004:10, 459–62,
491–92, 507, 510–11, **2006:**441,
485–86, 508–9, 534
do you celebrate, **2000:**417,
2003:452
enjoy it more if people did not
exchange gifts, **2000:**418
enjoy or not, **2000:**418
expect to take vacation during holidays, **2000:**429
expect to take vacation for how
many days during holidays,
2000:429
likely to use catalogs for shopping, **2000:**387
likely to use department stores for
shopping, **2000:**387, **2002:**370
likely to use discount stores for
shopping, **2000:**387, **2002:**370
likely to use Internet for shopping,
2000:388, **2002:**370
likely to use mail-order catalogues
for your shopping, **2002:**370
likely to use specialty stores for
shopping, **2000:**387, **2002:**370
open presents on Christmas
Day or Christmas Eve,
2003:452
prefer to receive gift you specifically asked for, or something
as a surprise, **2003:**452
spending on, **2003:**411
amount of, **2000:**387, **2001:**
263, **2003:**410–11, 451–52
versus last year, **2003:**411,
452
too commercialized, **2000:**418
too much emphasis on gifts,
2000:418
too much emphasis on religious
basis, **2000:**418
Chung, Connie, 2001:202–3

church, church attendance, 2004:
118–19, 255–56, 303–4, 329,
332–33, 358, 370, 506–7, 511–12,
2006:232–34, 2007:94, 269–71
abortion and, 2004:473–74
age and, 2004:303–4, 512,
2005:114
alcohol and, 2006:311
Bible and, 2007:230
Brownback, Sam, and,
2007:113–14, 326
Bush, George W., and,
2004:332–33, 442–43
Catholicism and, 2004:119, 329,
370, 512, 2005:131–32, 233,
2007:150
charitable giving and, 2006:60
Christianity and, 2005:233
Christmas and, 2005:477–78
Clark, Wesley, and, 2007:114
Clinton, Bill, and, 2005:183
confidence in, 2003:205–6,
2004:224–25, 251, 306,
2005:201
creationism and, 2004:463,
2005:191, 355
crime and, 2007:217
death penalty and, 2004:454–55,
495, 2005:186, 457
drugs and, 2005:408
Easter and, 2005:114
election of 2004 and,
2004:332–33, 442–43, 473–74,
2005:182
election of 2006 and, 2006:253,
355–56, 378, 424–26, 459–60,
465, 472
election of 2008 and, 2007:107–9,
113–15, 187–88, 253–54,
326–27, 423–24, 462–63,
471–72, 548
euthanasia and, 2005:179–80
evangelical Christianity and,
2005:233

evolution and, 2004:463–64,
2005:191, 355, 2007:250, 252
existentialism and, 2004:47
federal government and, 2006:256
frequency of, 2007:150
gambling and, 2004:123
gender and, 2003:205, 2004:304,
332–33, 506, 512, 2005:114,
2007:150
geographic region and, 2004:512,
2005:114
Gilmore, Jim, and, 2007:326
Gingrich, Newt, and,
2007:113–14, 187–88, 326
Giuliani, Rudy, and, 2007:113–14,
187–88, 253–54, 326, 548
Gonzales, Alberto, and, 2005:246
Gore, Al, and, 2005:183
government and, 2004:447, 505–7
guns and, 2004:464–65
Hagel, Chuck, and, 2007:326
happiness and, 2007:554
homelessness and, 2005:134
homosexuality and, 2005:142,
2007:233
Huckabee, Mike, and, 2007:326,
548
hunger and, 2005:134
Hunter, Duncan, and, 2007:326
ideology and, 2004:103
income and, 2004:512
Kerry, John, and, 2004:332–33,
442–43, 2005:182
law enforcement and, 2005:420
marriage amendment and,
2004:86–87, 202–3
marriage and, 2005:142
McCain, John, and, 2007:113–14,
187–88, 326–27, 548
morality and, 2004:13, 506–7,
2005:132, 2007:239
news and, 2006:59
Paul, Ron, and, 2007:326
personal lives and, 2006:143

political affiliation and, **2004:**93,
391–92, **2005:**182–84, 268,
2006:109–10, 124, 231–32,
253, 355–56, 368, 378,
424–26, 472
political power of, **2004:**505–7
poverty and, **2005:**134
Protestantism and, **2004:**370, 512,
2005:233, **2007:**150
race and, **2004:**303–4, 333, 512
religion and, **2005:**463,
2007:43–44, 94, 150
Romney, Mitt, and, **2007:**113–14,
187–88, 326, 548
satisfaction and, **2007:**554
Schiavo, Terri, and, **2005:**105
sex and, **2004:**490–91
stem cell research and, **2004:**415
suicide and, **2004:**281,
2005:179–80
Tancredo, Tom, and, **2007:**326
teenagers and, **2004:**47, 358, 370,
391–92, 490–91
Thompson, Fred, and,
2007:187–88, 326, 548
Thompson, Tommy, and,
2007:113–14, 326
traditional values and, **2004:**447
U.S., satisfaction with, by,
2006:81, 238
church activities
favorite way of spending an
evening, **2002:**6
hobby you are particularly interested in, **2002:**7
Churchill, Winston, 2004:230, 514,
2005:482
admiration of, **2000:**264,
2002:400
identified with what nation,
2000:141, 156
CIA (Central Intelligence Agency)
and assassination of President
Kennedy, **2003:**413

The Cider House Rules **(movie),**
2000:98
cigarette smoking and smokers,
2004:330–31, 417, **2005:**269–70,
301–3, 431, 442, 450
addicted to cigarettes (asked of
smokers), **2000:**394
age and, **2004:**79–80, 307
age you began smoking (asked of
smokers), **2000:**393
ban on, **2000:**394, **2003:**274,
2004:306–7, 417
blame for, **2000:**221, 394
cheating and, **2004:**192
children and, **2004:**80
civil liberties and, **2004:**307
Congress and, **2004:**417
discrimination and, **2002:**236,
2004:307, 330–31
discrimination on, **2003:**274
employment and, **2003:**274
ever smoke cigarettes regularly
[based on nonsmokers],
2002:236
gender and, **2004:**79, 307
as harmful, **2003:**269
health and, **2004:**417, 468, 476,
483
health ratings, smokers vs. non-
smokers, **2002:**5
higher health insurance rates justified for persons who smoke,
2003:275
how many do you smoke each day
(asked of smokers), **2000:**393,
2002:235–36
if you had to do it over again,
would you start smoking
(asked of smokers), **2000:**394
Medicaid and, **2004:**417
mortality and, **2004:**79
as most important issue, **2004:**183
opinion of, **2003:**269
parents and, **2004:**80

cigarette smoking and smokers
(continued)
policies concerning, **1998:**177,
2004:306–7
rates of, **2002:**236, **2004:**79–80, 417
respect you have for person who
smokes, **2003:**274
secondhand smoke, **2003:**269
Senate tobacco bill to reduce
number of teenagers who
smoke or raise revenue,
1998:185
should be made totally illegal,
2003:269–70
smoked in past week, **1998:**188,
2000:393, **2002:**4–5, 235,
2003:268–69, 274
taxes on, **1998:**177–78,
2002:236–37
teenagers and, **2004:**183
tobacco companies, **1998:**177–78,
185, **1999:**277, **2000:**221, 394
would you like to give up smoking
[based on smokers], **2002:**236
Cincinnati Inquirer
heard or read about its illegally
obtaining information on Chiquita Banana Co., **1998:**193–94
Cincinnati Reds, 2001:81
cities, 2004:448–50
prefer to live in city, suburban
area, small town, or on farm,
1998:238
See also urban areas
Citizen Kane (movie), **1998:**187
citizenship, 2006:136–38, 145–46,
203–4, 282
Civil Aeronautics Board, 2004:417
civil liberties, 2002:275, **2004:**19,
94–95, 112, 178, 307, **2005:**266,
374, 475–76
assessment of, **2006:**50
Bush, George W., and, **2002:**
275–76

election of 2006 and, **2006:**455
political affiliation and, **2006:**16,
455
See also human rights
Civil Rights Act, 1964
as most important event in twenti-
eth century, **2002:**175
civil rights movement
agree with goals of, **2000:**119
impact of, **2000:**119
civil unions, 2004:105–7, 201–2,
404–5, 442–43, **2005:**3–4, 38, 143
See also marriage
Civil War
states' rights as major issue in,
2000:141
clairvoyance
believe in, **2001:**137
Clapton, Eric, 2000:265
Clark, Wesley, 2005:300,
2006:235–36, 477, 531
church attendance and, **2007:**114
Democratic Party and, **2004:**34
economy and, **2004:**31, 33
education and, **2007:**354
election of 2004 and, **2004:**5–6,
11–12, 27–28, 30–34, 40–41,
48–49, 60–61, 76, **2007:**354
familiarity with, **2004:**48–49
gender and, **2004:**5–6, **2007:**124
healthcare and, **2004:**31
image of, **2004:**6, 43, 48–49
Iraq war and, **2004:**31–32
likely to support, **2003:**323,
335–36, 364, 374–75, 382,
390, 417, 432–33, 446–47
opinion of, **2003:**306
personal qualities of, **2004:**
32–34
as second choice for nomination,
2003:335
Clarke, Richard, 2004:134–35,
144–45, 394
class standing, 2004:47

claustrophobia
  fear of being closed in small
    space, **1998:**238, **2001:**70
Clemens, Roger, 1998:226,
  2007:531
Clemente, Roberto, 2001:83
clergy, 2004:13, 485, **2005:**125,
  448–49
  homosexuals should be hired as,
    1999:169
  honesty and ethical standards of,
    1999:148, **2000:**388,
    2001:265, **2002:**373, **2003:**422
  recommend as career for young
    man, **1998:**238
  See also ministers; priests
Cleveland Indians, 2001:81
Clinton, Bill
  admiration of, **1998:**1, 154, **1999:**
    242, **2000:**264, 431, **2001:**11,
    278, **2002:**399, **2003:**454,
    2004:513–14, **2005:**482
  age and, **2004:**205
  al Qaeda and, **2004:**134–35, 146,
    167–68
  approval ratings, **1998:**12–14, 17,
    23, 72–73, 91–92, 100–101,
    109–10, 126, 151–52, 197,
    202, 227, **1999:**12, 43, 91,
    95–96, **2000:**12, 262, 268, 335,
    363, 422, **2001:**11, 14, 31,
    2002:96, **2004:**8, 17, 104, 113,
    151, 205, 211–12, 229–32,
    247–49, 258–59, 265–66, 303,
    413–14, 416, 422, 444, 450,
    2005:24–27, 33–34, 49–51,
    118–19, 141, 263, 320,
    392–93, 397, **2006:**23–24,
    40–42, 53, 92, 96, 172, 182,
    190, 200–201, 245–46, 329,
    375, 434, 466, 539, **2007:**
    25–26, 166, 313, 484
  after two years in office (Dec.
    1994), **2002:**387

  averages during seventh quar-
    ter as president, **2002:**322
  in December of last year in
    office, *Gallup analysis* of,
    2000:422
  Gallup analysis of, **2000:**268
  volatility in, *Gallup analysis*
    of, **1998:**22–23
  bin Laden, Osama, and, **2004:**146
  budget and, **1998:**2, 55–56, 157,
    162, **1999:**44, 92, 142
  Bush, George W., and, **2001:**12,
    247, **2005:**425
  campaign finance and, **2006:**189
  characteristics of, **1998:**160, 173,
    202
  China and, **1998:**75–76, 81–83,
    86, 185
  church and, **2005:**183
  Clinton, Hillary, and, **2006:**304–5,
    332–33
  confidence in, **1998:**161, 199,
    201, 204, 240, **1999:**27, 31–32,
    2005:425
  Congress and, **1998:**202, 232,
    235
  as conservative or liberal,
    1998:158
  conventions and, **2004:**279–80,
    312, 356–57
  corporations and, **2002:**189
  crime and, **1999:**44, **2000:**262,
    2005:73, **2007:**38
  Democratic convention speech,
    2000:269
  Democratic Party and, **2004:**104,
    211–12, 229–30, 237–38, 319,
    514, **2007:**71–72, 88–89, 135
  dissatisfaction with, as most
    important issue, **1998:**60,
    1999:195
  dynasty and, **2007:**513
  economy and, **1998:**73, 202,
    1999:44, **2000:**170–71, 206,

261–62, 335, **2002:**223,
2004:258, **2005:**33
education and, **1998:**56–57,
1999:44, **2000:**262, **2007:**355
effective president in remaining
two years, **1998:**124, 250
election of, **2004:**17, 41–42, 85,
96, 113, 124–25, 151, 259,
265–66, 337–38
election of 1992 and, **2007:**21, 355
election of 2008 and,
2004:456–57
energy and, **2000:**334, **2001:**130
environment and, **1999:**44,
2006:141
equal pay laws for women and,
2000:43
ethics of, **2005:**399
familiarity with, **2004:**84
family issues handled by,
1998:202
foreign affairs and, **1998:**188,
202, **1999:**43, **2000:**171, 333,
335, **2005:**32, 34
fund-raising and, **1998:**167, 198,
204
Gallup analysis of gender gap,
versus Bush/Dole, **2000:**159
González, Elían, and, **2000:**104,
129, 131
Gore and, **1999:**58–59, **2000:**261,
352
government shutdown and,
1999:141
as greatest president, **2000:**58,
2001:44, **2003:**163–64, 413,
2004:233
healthcare and, **1999:**44, **2005:**73,
2007:38, 514
homelessness and, **1999:**44
honesty and ethical standards of,
1998:179, 197, 202, 215,
1999:47, **2001:**11, **2005:**300
human rights and, **1998:**81–82

image of, **2004:**233, 237–38,
247–49, **2005:**49, 76, 206
inauguration of, **2005:**24–25
independents and, **2004:**211–12,
229–30, 238, **2007:**71–72, 135
influence of, **1998:**160, 250
interested in hearing live speech
by, **2001:**79–80
investigation of, **2000:**195–96
Iraq and, **1998:**30–31, 33–34, 151,
167–70, 232, 251, **1999:**44
Kosovo and, **1999:**25, 31–32, 34,
36
legacy of, **1998:**203–4, **2000:**262,
2001:12, **2006:**518
like to see next president continue
with his policies, **1999:**95
marriage of, **2005:**301
media and, **1999:**15
Medicare and, **1998:**55, **1999:**44,
204, 218
Middle East and, **1998:**228
moderates and, **2004:**318
morality and, **1998:**124–25,
160–61, 174, 197, **2000:**262
opinion of, **1998:**14–15, 17, 27,
35–36, 110, 155, 160, 172–73,
199, 202–3, 213, 215–16,
247–48, 252, **1999:**12, 14, 44,
95, **2000:**262, 363, **2001:**41,
2006:42
other countries and, **2000:**171
as outstanding president,
1998:160, **1999:**77, **2000:**59
pardons and, **2001:**31, 63
perjury by, **2004:**54
personal life doesn't matter as
long as he does good job,
1998:204
plan for solving country's problems, **1998:**160
policies of, **2006:**45
political affiliation and,
2005:51–52, 398, 483,

2006:41–42, 172, 190, 246, 305, 401–2, 537, **2007:**71–72, 88–89, 135

post-White House, recommendations for, **2000:**188–89, **2001:**12

poverty and, **1999:**44

Puerto Rican nationalists and, **1999:**224

qualifications of, **1998:**160, 196, 202, 247, **1999:**47

race relations and, **1998:**180, 184, **1999:**44

re-election potential of, **2004:**8, 387

Republican Party and, **1998:**232, **1999:**92, **2004:**104, 211–12, 229–30, 237–38, 319, **2007:**71–72, 88–89, 135

resign and turn presidency over to Gore, **1998:**126, 131, 199, 229, 247, 249

September 11, 2001, terrorist attacks and, **2004:**145–46, 267

shares your values, **1998:**202, **1999:**47

should be charged with crime after he leaves office, **1999:**16

Social Security and, **1999:**44

State of the Union Address and, **1998:**161–62, **2004:**19, 28–29, **2005:**50–52, 73, **2006:**40–42, 45, **2007:**38

as success or failure as president, **1998:**159, 203, **2000:**262

supporter of, **2001:**11

swing voters and, **2004:**283

tax cuts and, **1999:**218

taxes and, **1998:**54–55, **1999:**44, 132, **2004:**154

terrorism and, **2004:**134–35

U.S., satisfaction with, and, **2004:**239, 341–42, 355

vote for Clinton, Dole, or Perot if you could vote in 1996 election again, **1998:**205

wasted opportunity to address important problems, **2000:**277

Whitewater and, **1998:**105–6, 179, 198

as worst president, **2000:**58

Yugoslavia and, **1999:**27, **2000:**333

See also Clinton impeachment controversy

Clinton, Hillary Rodham, 2004:456–57, 513–14

admiration of, **1998:**2, 154, 164, **1999:**242, **2000:**431, **2001:** 278, **2002:**400, **2003:**455, **2005:**483

age and, **2005:**81, **2007:**47, 124–25, 227–29, 253–54, 419, 423–24, 471–72, 547

approval ratings, **1998:**17–18, 27, 110–11, **1999:**44, **2000:**45, **2001:**1, **2007:**414

books by, **2003:**188, 196

characteristics of, **2003:**187

Clinton, Bill, and, **1998:**210, **2003:**196, **2006:**304–5, 332–33

conservatives and, **2007:**21, 33–34, 141–43, 227–29, 253–54, 423–24, 471–72, 547

Democratic Party and, **2005:**206

dynasty and, **2007:**513

in election match-ups, **2007:**68–69, 93, 132, 137, 170, 197, 202, 213–14, 242–43, 253–54, 267–69, 275–76, 285–86, 302, 311, 320–22, 399, 487–88, 505–6, 534–35, 538–40

election of 2000 and, **1998:**180–81

election of 2004 and, **2001:**192, **2002:**90, 395

election of 2008 and, **2003:**196,
  2005:80, 204–7, 288–90,
  299–301, 468
employment and, **2007:**301
familiarity with, **2007:**225–26,
  367–69, 388–89, 550
feelings about, **2003:**196
gender and, **2005:**80–82, **2006:**
  274–75, 301, 304–5, 537,
  2007:21, 47–48, 124–25,
  141–43, 227–29, 253, 398–99,
  419, 423–24, 471–72, 547
versus Gore, Al, **2006:**332–33
healthcare and, **2007:**46–48,
  287–89, 329–31, 432–33,
  469–71, 514
honesty of, **1998:**179, **2005:**300
ideology and, **2005:**207, 309
image of, **2005:**79–82, 204–7,
  288–89, 300–301, 309,
  2006:34–35, 273–75, 300–301,
  304–5, 330, 504–7, 532
and impeachment controversy,
  1998:160, 164–65, 201, 204,
  210, 248, **2003:**196
interested in hearing live speech
  by, **2001:**80
versus Kerry, John, **2006:**332–33
leadership of, **2005:**300
liberals and, **2007:**21, 33–34,
  141–43, 227–29, 253–54,
  423–24, 471–72, 547
marriage and, **2005:**81–82, 301
moderates and, **2007:**21, 33–34,
  141–43, 227–29, 253–54,
  423–24, 471–72, 547
opinion of, **1998:**155, 247, 252,
  1999:45, **2001:**1, 31,
  2003:187, 195–96
political affiliation and, **2005:**
  80–82, 289–90, 300–301, 309,
  483, **2006:**5, 34–35, 274–75,
  300–301, 305, 330, 332, 456,
  474, 532, 537

political ideology and, **2007:**21,
  33–34, 141–43, 227–29,
  253–54, 423–24, 471–72, 547
predictions for, **2003:**196, **2007:**1
Puerto Rican nationalists and,
  1999:224
qualifications of, **1999:**111,
  2003:187
Rumsfeld, Donald, and, **2006:**400
Senate run, **1999:**62, 111,
  2000:46
terrorism and, **2005:**301
values of, **2005:**300
Whitewater and, **1998:**179
Clinton impeachment controversy,
  2004:60, 147, 230, 247–48
allegations
  affair with Lewinsky, **1998:**6,
    92, 163, 203
  lied under oath about affair,
    1998:6, 92–93, 163–64,
    215, 235
  obstructed justice, **1998:**6–7,
    93, 164, 235
  sexual relations with any
    woman besides his wife or
    Lewinsky, **1998:**164
apologies and, **1998:**200, 206,
  209, 244
approval ratings, **1998:**126,
  130–31, 214
  factors affecting, **1998:**7, 188,
    200, 208–9, 215
attentiveness to, **1998:**5–6, 198,
  203, 246, 248
believe him, **1998:**167, 195, 208,
  217
betrayed public's trust, **1998:**203
blame for, **1998:**200–201, 215
cause in, **1998:**42
censure, **1998:**212
character of Clinton, **1998:**209
confidence in, **1998:**15–16,
  101–3

coverup of, **1998:**161, 167
Democrats and, **1998:**248
effectiveness as president,
  1998:124, 213, 250
effects of, **1998:**161, 245, **1999:**17
fairness in, **1998:**216, **1999:**9, 16
grand jury and, **1998:**199, 207–8,
  217, 244
hidden microphone and,
  1998:9–10
Hillary and, **1998:**210, 248
importance of, **1998:**245
influenced testimony in,
  1998:208, 243, **1999:**3–4, 9
investigation, **1998:**95, 182
Iraq and, **1998:**168
leaks and, **1998:**166–67
Lewinsky and, **1998:**8–9, 164,
  172, 196, 207–8
Livingston and, **1998:**251
media and, **1998:**18–19, 248
misused office, **1998:**243
nature of, **1998:**249
opinion of, **1998:**173, 177, 199,
  207, 217, 248
perjury and, **1998:**207–9, 217,
  243–44, **1999:**2–3, 9
privacy and, **1998:**199, 210, 217
relevance of, **1998:**7–8
remain in office, **1998:**131–32,
  199, 213, 216
removal from office, factors
  affecting, **1998:**104–5, 107
Republicans and, **1998:**248
resignation and, **1998:**126,
  131–32, 199, 213, 216, 229,
  247, 249
respect him, **1998:**210
right-wing conspiracy against
  him, **1998:**18, 179
Rose Garden statement [Dec. 11],
  1998:244
seriousness of, **1998:**197, 223,
  243, **1999:**4, 76

sexual relations only if two people
  have had intercourse, **1998:**216
situation has gotten out of hand,
  1998:215
speeches on, **1998:**161, 199–200,
  203
Starr report and, **1998:**207–8
State of the Union Address and,
  1998:161–62
support him, **1998:**164, 198, 200
testimony in, **1998:**94–95,
  199–200, 214, 216, 218
timing of, **1998:**176, 188–89, 198
as unfit to be president, **1998:**209
White House aides and,
  1998:208–9
witnesses in, **1998:**73–74, 167
cloning, 2004:250
of animals
  endangered species, **2002:**144
  as morally acceptable,
    2002:144, 150, **2003:**159
  pets, **2002:**144
  should be allowed, **2001:**136
Bush, George W., and,
  2002:145–46
human cells from adults, for medical research, **2002:**144
human embryos, for medical
  research, **2002:**144
human organs or body parts, for
  medical transplants, **2002:**144
of humans
  commonplace in year 2025,
    1998:221
  legal in year 2025, **1998:**221
  as morally acceptable,
    2002:145, 150, **2003:**159,
    218
  should be allowed, **2001:**136,
    2002:144
of stem cells, used for medical
  research morally acceptable,
  2002:145

Clooney, George, **2001**:76–77, **2003**:80, **2006**:191–92, 536
closed in a small place
fear of, **1998**:238, **2001**:70
clothing, 2004:305
race and, **2005**:274
sales of, **2005**:222
spending on, **2005**:86–87, 222, 367, 410
CNN, 2004:388
how often do you get your news from, **1998**:191
nerve gas story, **1998**:193–94
trust accuracy of news from, **1998**:97
coaches (of youth sports)
can be trusted, **2002**:199
Coalition Provisional Authority, 2004:173, 178, 210, 262–63
Coast Guard, 2002:152, **2004**:220–21
Cobb, David, 2004:378–79
Cobb, Ty, 1999:256, **2001**:83
cohabitation, 2004:103, 132
Cold War, 2004:97
Cole, Juan, 2004:493
Coleman, Gary, 2003:279
Cole (USS) situation, **2000**:343
collections
hobby you are particularly interested in, **2002**:7
college, 2007:371–3373
assessment of, **2006**:408
cost of, as most important issue, **2005**:45, 93–95, 113, 152–53, 198, 223, 366, 409, 421
income and, **2006**:483
race and, **2006**:484
See also education
College of American Pathologists, 2004:305
Collins, Susan, 2004:504
Colombia, 2000:174, **2001**:44, 84, **2002**:52, **2003**:56

Colorado, 2002:160, 340
Colorado Rockies, 2001:81
Columbia University, 2003:299
Columbine High School. *See* Littleton, Colorado, school shootings; Students (age 13 to 17), asked of
Columbus, Christopher
discovered America in what year, **2000**:141
combat experience, 2004:77
combat troops
favor women serving as, **2002**:3
comic strips
how often do you read, **2000**:48
your favorite "Peanuts" character, **2000**:48
community, 2005:254–55, **2006**:346
creationism and, **2004**:463
crime and, **2004**:478–79
drugs and, **2004**:55, **2005**:163–64
economy and, **2005**:108
education and, **2004**:377, 455
election of 2004 and, **2004**:442–43
euthanasia and, **2005**:179
gambling and, **2004**:123
guns and, **2004**:472
health and, **2004**:476
Internet and, **2004**:109
Kerry, John, and, **2004**:442–43
law enforcement and, **2005**:420
marriage and, **2004**:223
movies and, **2004**:89
Patriot Act and, **2004**:89
race and, **2004**:18–19, 223, 282
safety of, **2004**:448–50
satisfaction with, **2003**:360, **2004**:18–19, **2005**:11
school and, **2004**:305, 455
sex offenders in, **2005**:211–12
stress and, **2004**:182
suicide and, **2005**:179
community activities
importance in your life, **2003**:1

community groups
 support to parents from, **1998:**190
computer(s), 2004:154–55
 advancement of
  as most important issue,
   2001:59, 121, 256, **2002:**10
  as most important issue facing
   nation 25 years from now,
   2002:117
 children and, **1998:**189–90
 favorite way of spending evening,
  2002:6
 as favorite way of spending
  evening, **1998:**237
 hobby you are particularly interested in, **2002:**7
 as news source, **1998:**98, 193
 salesmen, honesty rating, **1999:**148
 use patterns, **1998:**185, 233,
  1999:145, **2003:**168
 violence and, **1999:**202–3
 viruses, **2000:**177–78
 See also e-mail; Internet;
  Microsoft Corporation; Y2K
  computer problem
computer industry, 2001:200,
 2002:240, **2003:**289
 confidence in, **1999:**210
 economy and, **2000:**206, **2002:**223
 executives, honesty rating, **1999:**148
 recommend as career for young
  man, **1998:**238
 recommend as career for young
  woman, **1998:**238–39, **2001:**109
 See also Microsoft Corporation
concern
 for abortion, **2004:**170, 428
 for accounting, **2004:**271–72
 for business, **2004:**147, 271–72
 for children, **2006:**495
 for corporations, **2004:**271–72
 for credit cards, **2004:**158,
  174–76, 207, **2005:**159,
  2006:167

 for crime, **2004:**120, 126–27,
  139, 159, 445–47, **2005:**136,
  162–64, 170–72, 391, **2007:**126
 for death, **2005:**117
 Democratic Party and, **2004:**127
 for drugs, **2004:**126–27, 139, 159,
  2007:126
 for economy, **2004:**10, 58, 64,
  120, 126–27, 159, **2007:**126
 for elections, **2004:**147, 412–13,
  422, 430–31, 433–34, 438–39
 for employment, **2004:**10, 58, 64,
  126–27, 159, 271–72, 340–41,
  343
 for energy, **2004:**120–22, 126–27,
  129–31, 139, 159, 271–72
 for environment, **2004:**126–27,
  131, 138–42, 158–61
 for federal budget, **2004:**58, 147,
  271–72
 for finances, **2004:**174–77, 206–7
 for foreign trade, **2004:**58
 for gasoline, **2004:**147–48,
  271–72, 424–25
 for government, **2004:**147
 for healthcare, **2004:**10, 26–27,
  64, 120, 126–27, 147, 159,
  174–75, 177, 207, 458–59
 for homelessness, **2004:**126–27,
  159, **2007:**126
 for housing, **2005:**159
 for hunger, **2004:**126–27, 159,
  2007:126
 for immigration, **2004:**21,
  126–27, 159, **2007:**126
 for impeachment, **2004:**147
 for inflation, **2004:**58
 for interest rates, **2004:**58
 investors and, **2004:**271–72
 for Iraq, **2004:**64, 147, 271
 for Islamic/Western relations,
  2006:118
 for mad cow disease, **2004:**8–9,
  147

concern *(continued)*
for Medicare, **2004:**147
for money, **2005:**159
for morality, **2004:**214
for North Korea, **2004:**147
for nuclear weapons and, **2006:**38
for outsourcing, **2004:**271–72, 343
parents and, **2006:**495
for poverty, **2004:**139
for race relations, **2004:**126–27,
139, 159, **2007:**126
Republican Party and, **2004:**127
for retirement, **2004:**174–75,
206–7, **2005:**159
for Social Security, **2004:**147
for standard of living, **2004:**10,
174–77, 207, **2005:**159
for stock market, **2004:**147
for taxes, **2004:**58
for television, **2006:**495
for terrorism, **2004:**20, 64, 120,
126–27, 159, 362–63, 446,
2005:18–20, 127–28, 136,
162–63, 170–72, 226–27, 251,
272–73, 293–94, 391, **2007:**126
for violence, **2004:**126–27, 159,
2007:126
See also issues, most important
Condit, Gary
approval ratings, **2001:**203
concerned about Chandra Levy
and her family, **2001:**202
did he lie at any point during these
interviews, **2001:**203–4
did his letter to you make you feel
more or less favorably toward
him, **2001:**204
embarrassed he represents your
district, **2001:**203
interviews and, **2001:**202–4
justified in not answering questions about his relationship
with Chandra Levy, **2001:**203,
2001:204

likely he was directly involved in
disappearance of Chandra
Levy, **2001:**165, 188, 202–3
media and, **2001:**204
opinion of, **2001:**202–3
should apologize to constituents
or to the Levy family,
2001:204
should resign from Congress
immediately, **2001:**188
should take a lie detector test
about disappearance of Chandra Levy, **2001:**165
support for, **2001:**203, 205
Confederate flag, 2000:145
**Conference of Catholic Bishops,
2004:**13–14, 251
confidence
in American Civil Liberties
Union, **2004:**94
in Ashcroft, John, **2004:**94
in banks, **2004:**224, 306,
2005:201
in Bush, George W., **2004:**29,
2006:39, 62, **2007:**204–5,
306–7, 393, 418
in business, **2004:**225, 306,
2005:201
in church, **2004:**224–25, 251, 306,
2005:201
in Congress, **2004:**225, 306,
2005:172–73, 201–2,
2006:39, 188–89, 227,
232–34, 411, **2007:**204–5,
269–71, 393, 418
of consumers, **2004:**9–11,
150–51, 235–37, 285–86
in criminal justice system,
2004:225, 306
in defense, **2004:**167–68, 224–25,
251, 306
in Democratic Party,
2004:386–87, **2007:**204–5,
393

in economy, **2004:**9–13, 20,
23–25, 35–36, 69–70, 78,
107–8, 125, 150–51, 189–91,
235–37, 246–47, 254–55,
285–86, 333–35, 359, 379–81,
451–53, 491–92, 507–9
in employment, **2004:**35, 39, 107,
110, 152–53, 235–36, 242–43,
276–77, 286, 340–41, 451–52,
508
in federal government, **2006:**76
in food safety, **2006:**522
in Greenspan, Alan, **2006:**39
in healthcare, **2004:**225, **2005:**201
in HMOs, **2004:**225, 306,
2005:201
in housing, **2004:**277
in intelligence system, **2004:**53,
167–68
in Iraq, **2007:**393
in Joint Chiefs of Staff, **2007:**393
in journalists, **2005:**201–2
in judicial system, **2005:**201–2
in labor, **2004:**225, 306
in labor unions, **2005:**201–2
in law enforcement, **2004:**81,
224–25, 251, 306
in media, **2004:**163–64, 225, 306,
387–88, 392–94, **2005:**201–2,
357
in Medicare, **2004:**306
in military, **2005:**201, 229,
2006:232–33, 411
in NASA, **2005:**250
in national defense, **2007:**269–71,
393
in national security, **2004:**167–68
in news, **2005:**201–2, 357
in newspapers, **2004:**225, 306,
2005:201–2
in Petraeus, David, **2007:**393
in political parties, **2006:**39
in presidency, **2004:**224–25, 306,
2005:201–2

in religion, **2004:**13, 224–25, 251,
306, **2005:**201–2
in Republican Party,
2004:386–87, **2007:**204–5,
393
in schools, **2004:**225, 305–6,
2005:201
in stock market, **2004:**451–52
in Supreme Court, **2004:**225, 306,
2007:269–71, 418
in television, **2004:**225, 306
terrorism and, **2004:**167–68
in United Nations, **2006:**62
in voting systems, **2004:**315–16
in weight loss, **2004:**149
See also trust
Congress
age and, **2004:**205–6, **2005:**145,
330, **2007:**91
and anthrax, **2001:**238
approval ratings, **1998:**25,
132–33, 247, **1999:**47,
2000:12, 368, **2001:**13, 145,
186, 199, 232, 254, **2002:**173,
270–71, 344, 382, **2003:**325,
387–88, **2004:**68–69, 205–6,
450–51, **2005:**98, 144–45,
169–70, 212–14, 330, 384–85,
396–97, 412, 430, **2007:**38–39,
53, 118–19, 153, 201–2,
210–11, 266–67, 271–72,
322–23, 364–65, 384–85,
408–9, 418, 441–42, 494–95,
501–2, 529
baseball and, **2004:**488
and China, **1998:**76
China and, **2000:**124
and cigarettes, **1998:**177
Clinton and, **1998:**202
confidence in, **1998:**181, 240,
253, **1999:**50, 141–42, 209,
2000:121, 209, 216, **2001:**3,
149, **2002:**185, 282,
2003:205–6, 355–56, 388,

Congress *(continued)*

2004:163–64, 205, 225, 306,
2005:172–73, 201–2, 359, 378,
2006:39, 188–89, 227, 232–34,
398, 411, 514, 2007:204–5,
269–71, 393, 415, 418

constituents and, 2006:14, 318

corruption and, 2006:4–6, 13–15,
188–89, 204–6, 226–28,
458–60, 478, 2007:16–17,
60–61, 305

defense spending and, 2004:97

Democratic Party and, 1998:227,
2002:16, 46, 89–90, 101–2,
171, 186–87, 273–74,
2003:415, 2004:68–69, 205,
435–36, 451, 2007:16–17, 39,
53–55, 66–67, 118–19, 153,
210–11, 267, 322–23, 364–65,
408, 441–42, 494–95, 502

and Department of Homeland
Security, 2002:351

dissatisfaction with, as most
important issue, 2001:121,
2002:10, 71, 116, 233, 360,
2003:25, 62, 86, 122, 155, 203,
284, 401, 443

economy and, 2000:206, 262, 2001:
275, 2003:17–18, 321, 2005:
3–4, 65–67, 130, 172–73, 412

education and, 2004:164,
2005:3–4, 65–67, 144,
2007:60–61, 90, 191–92,
237–38, 305

employment and, 2007:60–61,
191–92, 237–38, 305, 385

energy and, 2007:16–17, 60–61,
237–38, 305

environment and, 2007:60–61, 90,
191–92, 237–38, 305

equal pay laws for women,
2000:43

foreign affairs and, 2007:60–61,
90, 237–38, 305

foreign aid and, 2007:60–61,
237–38, 305

gasoline and, 2005:130, 325, 412,
422, 2007:60–61, 90, 191–92,
237–38, 305

gender and, 2003:205, 2005:145,
2007:91

Gingrich and, 1998:232

González, Elían, and, 2000:132,
138

government and, 2005:412

healthcare and, 2005:3–4, 65–67,
130, 412

homelessness and, 2007:60–61,
237–38, 305

homosexuality and, 2004:369

hunger and, 2007:60–61, 237–38,
305

Hurricane Katrina and, 2005:337,
343, 353

and impeachment controversy
approval ratings, 1998:164,
196, 229, 249, 1999:16
attentiveness to, 1998:148–49,
214, 243–44, 246, 248
censure in, 1998:126–27, 210,
213, 229, 242, 244, 247
confidence in, 1998:216–17,
234
constituents and, 1998:211,
246
Democrats and, 1998:245
effects of, 1998:245–47
fairness of, 1998:223, 1999:16
feelings about, 1998:242, 246
hearings, 1998:120–21,
123–24, 130, 211, 231
House and, 1998:218, 244, 247
House Judiciary Committee
and, 1998:149–50, 223, 235
investigation of, 1998:206
opinion of, 1998:211–12, 248
perjury and, 1998:173–74
as priority, 1998:231, 236

public opinion and, **1998:**209
Republicans and, **1998:**244–45
resignation and, **1998:**247
Senate and, **1998:**218, 244,
    249–50
Starr report, **1998:**119–20,
    210, 214, 234
testimony by Clinton,
    1998:214
timing of, **1998:**210
Willey, Kathleen, and,
    1998:173
as worthwhile, **1998:**234–35
your Congressperson and,
    1998:122–23, 212–13, 249
income and, **2005:**144
independents and, **2004:**68, 436,
    2007:16–17, 39, 53–55, 66–67,
    118–19, 153, 210–11, 267,
    322–23, 364–65, 408, 441–42,
    502
influence of, **2001:**37
Iraq and, **1998:**169, **2002:**279,
    285, **2005:**3–4, 65–67, 412,
    2006:107–8, 168–69, 227,
    268–69, 394–95, 409–11,
    458–60, 478, 500–501, 514
judicial system and, **2005:**130,
    2007:60–61, 305
and Kosovo, **1999:**27
leadership and, **2007:**60–61, 305
lobbying and, **2005:**170
marriage and, **2004:**369
Medicare and, **2004:**137–38, 394,
    2007:16–17, 60–61, 90,
    237–38, 305
members of
    honesty and ethical standards
        of, **1999:**148, **2000:**389,
        2001:265, **2002:**373,
        2003:422–23,
        2004:484–85, **2005:**448,
        2006:520
and Microsoft, **1998:**51–52

Middle East and, **2007:**237–38,
    305
military and, **2005:**209
morality and, **2005:**130
as most important issue,
    2004:37–38, 467, **2005:**99,
    174, 213, 348
national security and, **2005:**334,
    2007:60–61, 90, 191–92,
    237–38, 305
and nicotine, **1998:**177
oil and, **2007:**60–61, 90, 191–92,
    237–38, 305
and patients' bill of rights,
    2001:144
plans for, **2006:**448–50, 478
political affiliation and, **2005:**98,
    144, 169–70, 172–73, 202,
    214, 330, 360, 396–98,
    411–12, 429–31, 453,
    2007:16–17, 39, 53–55, 66–67,
    118–19, 153, 210–11, 267,
    322–23, 364–65, 408, 441–42,
    502
poverty and, **2007:**60–61, 179–80,
    237–38, 305
predictions for, **2001:**141,
    2002:388, **2003:**5, **2007:**1
prescription drugs and, **2006:**478
president and, **1998:**175
priorities for, **1998:**235–36,
    1999:98, **2001:**141, 229,
    2002:130, **2004:**40, **2007:**2–3,
    16–17, 60–61, 90–92, 148–49,
    191–92, 237–38, 305, 349
race and, **2005:**3–4, 145
Republican Party and, **1998:**227,
    2002:16, 46, 89–90, 101–2,
    171, 186–87, 273–74,
    2003:415, **2004:**68–69, 205,
    231, 435–36, 451, **2007:**16–17,
    39, 53–55, 66–67, 118–19,
    153, 210–11, 267, 322–23,
    364–65, 408, 441–42, 502

Congress *(continued)*
    Schiavo, Terri, and, **2005:**105,
        109–10, 112, 122–23, 145
    September 11, 2001, terrorist
        attacks and, **2004:**205, 325–26
    Social Security and, **1998:**194,
        2005:3–4, 34–36, 63, 65–67,
        130, 240, 412, **2007:**16–17,
        60–61, 90, 191–92, 237–38, 305
    Speaker of House of Representa-
        tives, name of, **2000:**34
    special interest groups and,
        2006:5, 14
    stem cell research and, **2005:**306
    as success or failure, **1998:**175
    taxes and, **1998:**177, **2005:**3–4, 6–7,
        37–38, 65–67, 412, **2006:**153,
        168–69, 409, 458–60, 478, **2007:**
        60–61, 191–92, 237–38, 305
    teenagers and, **2004:**440
    terrorism and, **2005:**3–4, 65–67,
        130, 334, 412
    tobacco issues, **1998:**177–78, 185,
        2004:417
    unemployment and, **2007:**60–61,
        191–92, 237–38, 305
    voting issues for, **2002:**306
    wages and, **2007:**385
Congressional elections,
    2004:327–28, 366–67, 435–36
    budget deficit and, **1998:**159
    Bush, George W., and, **2002:**338
    campaign finance reform and,
        1999:129
    campaigns, quality of, **1998:**227,
        2002:343–44
    change for the better if present
        members replaced with new
        members, **2002:**343
    crime and, **1998:**159, 225
    definitely will vote for Republican
        or Democrat, or possibly
        change mind before election,
        2002:311–12

economy and, **1998:**159, 225,
    2002:284, 290, 335–36
education and, **1998:**225
enthusiastic about voting,
    1998:227
environment and, **1998:**225
foreign affairs and, **1998:**225
generic ballots, **1998:**58–59, 114,
    128–29, 134, 139
gun control and, **1999:**132
healthcare and, **1998:**217, 225,
    1999:131
impeachment and, **1998:**123,
    217–18, 224–25, 227, 249
and investment climate, **2002:**344
Iraq and, **2002:**279, 284, 290, 307,
    335–36
issues in, **2002:**291, 312
matters great deal which political
    party controls Congress,
    2002:312
Medicare and, **1998:**159,
    1999:132
morality and, **1998:**218
pleased with selection of candi-
    dates running for Democratic
    nomination for president,
    2002:395
predictions for, **2002:**330
reelections, opinion of,
    1998:134–36, **2002:**290, 343
Republican Party and, **2002:**376
satisfaction with, **1998:**227,
    2002:343
Social Security and, **1998:**217,
    225
tax cuts and, **1998:**159, 217, 225,
    1999:131
taxes and, **1999:**218
vote for Democratic or Republi-
    can Party's candidate, **1998:**58,
    112–15, 128, 133–34, 139,
    141, 185, 201, **1999:**114,
    2000:16–17, 237, 272, 283,

371, **2002:**16, 288, 311, 319, 329–30, 338
Connecticut, 2006:364
Connery, Sean, 2000:98, **2001:**76
Conservative Party, 2004:57, 81
conservatives
  abortion and, **2004:**250, 473–74, **2005:**245–46, 260, 405–6, 443–44, **2007:**295
  age and, **2004:**103
  animals and, **2004:**250
  approval ratings and, **2004:**184, **2005:**144–45, 417
  automobile ownership and, **2004:**441
  blogs and, **2005:**98
  Bush, George W., and, **2000:**196, **2004:**102–3, 133, 184, 318–20, 441–42, **2005:**309–10, 417
  Bush, George W., and, **2000:**248
  business and, **2007:**8
  CBS News National Guard story and, **2004:**394
  church and, **2004:**103
  Clinton, Bill, and, **1998:**158
  Clinton, Hillary, and, **2005:**309, **2007:**21, 33–34, 141–43, 227–29, 253–54, 423–24, 471–72, 547
  cloning and, **2004:**250
  creationism and, **2004:**463, **2005:**191
  crime and, **2007:**217
  death penalty and, **2004:**250, 453, 495, **2005:**186, 457
  defense and, **2004:**98, 269
  Democratic Party and, **1998:**158, 231, **2004:**103
  divorce and, **2004:**250
  Dole, Bob, as, **2004:**319
  drugs and, **2005:**408
  economy and, **2004:**102–3, 269, **2005:**108, **2007:**295
  education and, **2006:**357

  election of 2004 and, **2004:**102–3, 424, 441–42, 473–74
  election of 2006 and, **2006:**253, 378, 470
  election of 2008 and, **2005:**310, **2007:**21, 33–34, 77–78, 107–9, 117–18, 141–43, 186–87, 227–29, 253–54, 294–96, 423–24, 462–63, 471–72, 546–48
  employment and, **2004:**345
  euthanasia and, **2005:**179–80
  evolution and, **2004:**464, **2005:**191
  family values and, **2007:**546
  federal government and, **2006:**256
  foreign affairs and, **2004:**102
  gambling and, **2004:**123, 250
  gasoline and, **2006:**186
  gender and, **2004:**103
  geographic region and, **2004:**103
  ghosts and, **2005:**253
  Giuliani, Rudy, and, **2007:**117–18, 186–87, 253–54, 294–96, 548
  Gonzales, Alberto, and, **2005:**246
  Gore and, **2000:**248
  government and, **2004:**269, 447, **2007:**8
  government surveillance and, **2006:**66
  guns and, **2004:**472, **2005:**141
  homelessness and, **2005:**134
  homosexuality and, **2004:**250, 505
  Huckabee, Mike, and, **2007:**548
  hunger and, **2005:**134
  Hunter, Duncan, and, **2007:**118
  identification with, **2004:**102–3
  immigration and, **2007:**113
  income and, **2004:**103
  independents and, **2004:**103
  Iraq war and, **2005:**244
  Kerry, John, and, **2004:**441–42

conservatives *(continued)*
  labor unions and, **2007:**8
  law enforcement and, **2005:**420
  marriage and, **2004:**86, 103
  McCain, John, and, **2007:**117–18,
    186–87, 548
  media and, **1998:**170–71,
    2004:388
  Middle East and, **2006:**122–23
  morality and, **2004:**250, **2006:**
    214, 219–20, 256, **2007:**239
  Mormonism and, **2007:**94
  music and, **2004:**441
  Nader, Ralph, and, **2004:**87
  Obama, Barack, and, **2007:**21,
    227–29, 462–63, 547
  Patriot Act and, **2004:**94
  patriotism and, **2005:**62
  Pelosi, Nancy, and, **2006:**499
  political affiliation and, **2006:**253,
    378, 446, 470
  poverty and, **2005:**134
  presidency and, **2004:**269
  Reid, Harry, and, **2006:**500
  religion and, **2004:**120, 512,
    2005:133, 151, 234, 448,
    2007:77–78, 94
  Republican Party and, **1998:**158,
    231, **2004:**103, 354
  Romney, Mitt, and, **2007:**117–18,
    186–87, 548
  Schiavo, Terri, and, **2005:**105
  September 11, 2001, terrorist
    attacks and, **2007:**395
  sex and, **2004:**250
  social problems and, **2004:**
    102–3
  suicide and, **2004:**250,
    2005:179–80
  Tancredo, Tom, and, **2007:**118
  taxes and, **2006:**153
  Thompson, Fred, and,
    2007:186–87, 548
  on threats, most critical, **2007:**8

  traditional values and, **2004:**57,
    447
  United Nations and, **2004:**102
  U.S., satisfaction with, **2006:**81,
    238
Constitution, 2006:208, 307
  amendments to
    and electoral reform, **2000:**375
    and flag burning, **1999:**262
    on marriage, **2004:**85–87,
      105–6, 201–3, 369, 371,
      471
  First Amendment as document
    guaranteeing free press,
    2000:141
  if signers of Declaration of Inde-
    pendence were alive, would
    they agree with way Constitu-
    tion is followed today,
    1999:206
  presidential election situation as
    constitutional crisis, **2000:**
    373–74, 382, 390, 396, 412
  rights under
    confessions obtained from
      defendants not read,
      2000:200
    inform person when arrested
      of, **2000:**200
  voter turnout and, **2004:**438
Constitution Party, 2004:349,
  378–79
consumers
  confidence of, **2004:**9–11,
    150–51, 235–37, 285–86
  credit cards and, **2004:**157–58
  economy and, **2004:**64, 107–8,
    150–51, 285–86, 451–53,
    491–92, 507–9
  employment and, **2004:**110–11,
    286, 508
  gasoline and, **2004:**148, 150–51,
    286
  globalization and, **2004:**508–9